Anonymous

Roster of Indiana Soldiers in the State of Kansas

Anonymous

Roster of Indiana Soldiers in the State of Kansas

ISBN/EAN: 9783337307301

Printed in Europe, USA, Canada, Australia, Japan

Cover: Foto ©Suzi / pixelio.de

More available books at **www.hansebooks.com**

ROSTER

— OF —

Indiana Soldiers,

IN THE

STATE OF KANSAS.

∴ ∴ ∴

COMPILED FROM RECORDS IN ADJU-
TANT GENERAL'S OFFICE AND
REUNION REGISTERS.

Numerically Arranged

: REGIMENTS, IN ALPHABETICAL ORDER, WITH
RANK, COMPANY, AND POST OFFICE AD-
DRESS, SO FAR AS KNOWN.

—ALSO—

AMES OF COLONELS OF REGIMENTS,

AND TERMS OF SERVICE.

∴ ∴ ∴ ∴ ∴ ∴ ∴ ∴ ∴

☞ Published by order of the Indiana Veteran Association of the War of the Rebellion
of the State of Kansas.

T. W. DURHAM, Sec'y.

TOPEKA, KAN., OCT. 1, 1888.

To the Indiana Veteran Association of the State of Kansas:

In obedience to instructions of the Association at their last meeting, held at Emporia Oct. 7th, 1888, I have prepared and published the Roster of Indiana Soldiers resident of Kansas. The records of the Adjutant General's office have furnished the greater part of the names. Registry books of reunions have also been searched and names and addresses have been learned from individuals and by correspondence. Names have been compared with the muster rolls in the report of Adjutant Terrell of Indiana to avoid errors, and thus hundreds of corrections have been made. Still there are doubtless many mistakes, but in the main it is correct. As to the addresses, however, they cannot be altogether relied on, for the soldier, like a bird, does not always remain where first he settles. The addresses published if not now correct will give a clue to trace from and may thus lead to the present address.

The work has been prepared with care, and the arrangement is in the most approved style, the Regiments being placed in numerical and the names of the men in alphabetical order, giving company and rank if known.

The work of preparing this Roster has been a labor of love, and it is the desire of the author that the work may prove interesting and useful and go far towards perfecting the spirit of Fraternity, Charity and Loyalty which should ever be found to exist between those who together fought and conquered the element of disunion. Dear to each patriot's heart should be the name and fame of every other patriot, and especially dear those of our own glorious old state, INDIANA

There having been no fund provided for publication, there appeared no other way to have the Roster printed, than for the Secretary to become personally responsible, and to advance a large part of the pay, and for his remuneration to look to the appreciation of his comrades of the association, in buying a sufficient number of the books to pay the costs of the publication. The number of Rosters printed being limited, it is hoped that all desiring will secure copies at once, before the edition is exhausted.

Respectfully submitted,

T. W. DURHAM, Secretary.

Muster Roll Indiana Veterans in Kansas.

NOTE—The order of arrangement is: first, by regiments; Indiana having furnished five regiments for the Mexican war, the number of the first regiment for the war of 1861 was the sixth; the regiments including infantry, cavalry and heavy artillery were numbered consecutively from six to one hundred and fifty-six.

There were thirteen regiments of cavalry and one of heavy artillery; regiment twenty-one was the first heavy artillery.

The 1st cavalry was	the	28th.	
" 2d	"	" "	41st.
" 3d	"	" "	45th.
" 4th	"	" "	77th.
" 5th	"	" "	90th.
" 6th	"	" "	71st.
" 7th	"	" "	119th.
" 8th	"	" "	59th.
" 9th	"	" "	121st.
" 10th	"	" "	125th.
" 11th	"	" "	126th.
" 12th	"	" "	127th.
" 13th	"	" "	131st.

The remaining regiments were infantry. The light artillery were designated as batteries by numbers from one to twenty-eight—the last number being colored.

Second, names are placed in alphabetical order—first, name; second, rank; third, company letter; fourth, postoffice address—all postoffices, unless otherwise noted, being in Kansas.

Where no rank is given it will be understood that the soldier was a private or that rank was unknown.

The usual military abbreviations have been used for rank, and also s for sergeant, c for corporal, m for musician.

SIXTH INFANTRY—3 MONTHS AND 3 YEARS.
Cols. T. T. Crittenden, P. P. Baldwin, H. Tripp.

Alford, J. W., E,	Erie
Allen, James, E,	Star Valley
Allison, Robt , lt., F,	Winfield
Anderson, H. H., D,	Maple City
Anderson. T. W., A,	Louisville
Auld, A. M.. C,	Blendon
Bales, M.. I,	Chapman
Boyle, J. G., C,	Eureka
Brown, V. A., C,	Red Stone
Brown, G. W., capt., K,	Scranton
Clearwater, R., s, A,	Hutchinson
Cory, G. W., F,	Jetmore
Craig, J. T., I,	Clearwater
David, D., C,	Norway
Day, D. D., B,	Blue Mound
Dike, W. H. F,	Aliceville
Dollar, D., K,	Paola
Ensminger, W. P., D,	Nickerson
Everroad, Geo., G,	Newark
Flora, D. S., E, .	McPherson
Fish, J. F., H,	Concordia
Fowle, Dixon, C,	Wilson
George, W.. I,	Erie
Hammond, J. D., K,	Burlington
Harris, W. P., D,	Lapland
Hendricks, C., c, G,	Concordia
Hersekill, F., I,	Pittsburg
Hobbs, W., B,	Emporia
Holeman, G. W., C,	Box City
Hopkins, W. C., s E,	Solomon

Hostatler, J. J., K,	W. Moreland
Howe, S. R., C,	Newark
Huffman, R , G,	Glen Sherrald
Hull, Jacob, A,	Moline
Huston, J. W., G,	Independence
Hutchinson, C. R , C,	Pleasant Green
Keith, J. W., G,	Manhattan
King, I. W., C,	Minneapolis
Kirkham, J. D., K,	Nickerson
Lawrence, T. F., E,	Oswego
Leasure, J. B., C,	Larned
Lucky, James, C,	Glen Elder
Lucky, J. M., c C,	Bulls City
Lund, Thos., A,	Glen Elder
McCullough, H., D,	Burlington
McDermit, J., D,	Cleardale
McLin, Wm., E,	Western Park
Ogden, J. D., B,	Independence
Palmer, O. H., c H,	Severy
Rigg, J. B., s I,	Delphos
Robinson, S. A., drum major,	Logan
Sampson, J. O., C,	Armistead
Smitn, W., K,	Fawn Creek
Smith, A. J., F,	Trading Post
Smith, Geo., A,	Randall
Stevens, J. M., m A,	Atchison
Thacker, J. W., A,	Augusta
Thompson, W. F., s I,	Farlinville
Thorn, W. S., c K,	Altoona
Tull, Isom, B,	Zeandale
Turk, A.,	Farlinville
Tuttle, L. C., H,	Leavenworth
Vantrees, H. E., lt E,	Sun City
Vessells, E., E,	Castleton
Vorhis, J. H., H,	Toronto
Ward, D. R., C,	Ellinwood
Ward, M., C,	Ellinwood
Worley, J. T., C,	Haddam
York, Caswell, B,	Kansas City, Kan.

SEVENTH INFANTRY—3 MONTHS AND 3 YEARS

Cols. E. Dumont, James Gaven, Ira G. Grover.

Alden, J. P., K,	Monmouth
Allison, W. G., F,	Iola
Barnhill, J. S., I,	Altoona
Bird, Jas. I,	Ft. Scott
Black, Joseph, B,	Wall Street
Branham, J. N., H,	Topeka
Bright, Sam, E,	Wilmington
Brown, H. A,	Coffeyville
Buchanan, S. A,	Irving
Burdette, Jas., E,	Nickerson
Burke, J. S., H,	Peabody
Burns, G. W., C,	Kiowa
Call, S. c s,	Elgin
Campbell, W. M., c, K,	Vosburg
Canary, A. J., F,	Independence
Cassidea, D., H,	Fontana
Clark, T. J., I,	Osborne
Cole, S. R., A,	Waseca
Cooper, W. M., C,	Melvern
Craig, L. S., s, D,	Wall Street
Cooksen, E., C,	Winfield
Curtis, B. M., 1st Lt., H,	Topeka
Davis, Wm., Lt., F,	Iola
Dodson, P. M., H,	Waverly
Dooley, H., B,	Neodesha
Dunlap, J. R., F,	Carlyle
Ferguson, J. E., D,	Delphos
Forgen, John, F;	Winfield
Freeman, R. C., c B,	Mulberry Grove
Garr, L. P., F,	Independence
Gentry, R. A., s, D,	Delphos
Glenn, J. W., C,	Sedan

Gresham, J. L., C,   Huron
Griffith, Isaac, Sgt., B,   Mound City
Harbert, S. T., I,   Mill Creek
Hodden, K. D., C,   Elmdale
Harding, J. L., s, I,   Louisburg
Harshberger, Wm., B,   Fredonia
Hay, J. M., F,   Wichita
Hess, W. M., G,   Topeka
Holman, L., G,   Lebo
Horton, C. S., D,   Harveysville
Houston, J. C., C,   Walnut
Hubble, Spence, H,   Mound Valley,
Huron G. H , s, I,   Topeka
Huston, W. D., A,   Altamont
Irey, W. S., I,   Mill Creek
Johnson, W. R., I,   Neodesha
Johnson, M., H,   Winfield
Jones, Thos., D,   Glasco
Jones, H. F., I,   Melvern
Jones, S. H., A,   Pleasant Run
Kester, W., H,   Salina
Kersey, J. H., G,   Judson
Knight, Henry, Lt., D,   Union Star Mo
Lawrence, D. R., G,   Lyons
Lovell, G. W., H,   Kingman
Loyd, G. P., E,   Sedan
Marsh, W., B,   Holden, Mo
Mechem, A. E., I,   Sterling
Meek, J. C., Capt., G,   Idana
McLin, J., K,   Garfield
Meredith, F., K,   Nickerson
Monroe, G., E,   Wicnita
Murphy, A. L., A,   Sterling
Neiman, M., C,   Millwood
Noggle. D. C., F,   Mapleton
Odell, H. C., K,   Leon
Orner, T. F. Lt., K,   Topeka
Orner, S. O., s K,   Topeka
Parr, S. P., E,   Columbus
Piper, R. H., D,   Elk City
Pryor, H., E,   Plainville
Pugh, T. J., sgt., I,   Hutchinson
Shives, J. Q. A., I,   Iuka
Simonton, S. S., C,   Topeka
Simonton, C. A., H,   Topeka
Smith, D. M., sgt., D,   Wyandotte
Smith, H. J., A,   Burrton
Stults, W. J., F,   Bennington
Surface, J. M., F,   Lake City
Temple, L., c. C,   Elm Valley
Thompson, R. J., A,   Cawker City
Throop, N., D,   Winfield
Vannuys, J. H., I,   Iola
Walker. J. M., A,   Kingman
Weigand, J.,   Peters
Wilkinson, J., G,   Lyons
Willard, J. S., sgt., E,   Hutchinson
Williams, C. M., G,   Lansing

EIGHTH INFANTRY, 3 MONTHS, 3 YEARS
AND VETERANS.
Cols, W. P. Benton, D. Shunk, J. B. Polk.

Armstrong, W. C., D,   Halstead
Baird, Wm., C,   Vesper
Bock, J. H., E,   Sulphur Springs
Bolinger, L., G,   Eldorado
Brittain, G., lt., C,   Garden City
Calkins, H., capt., C,   Independence
Carr, Mills, H,   Ionia
Chapman, A. B., K,   Benton
Chapman, M. V., G,   Le Roy
Cooper, S. V., C,   Morse
Cooper, Wm., B,   Melvern
Curry, R., C,   McCune
Cusick, L. S.,   H,   Girard

Name	Co.	Location
Dunkin, A. D.,	E,	Circleville
Dye, Fred.,	I,	Cloverdale
Earhart, L.,	A,	Emporia
Edwards, W. J.,	H,	Galena
Ellis, B. F.,	R,	Crane
Fagan, W. F.,	C,	Topeka
Fessler, Wm. H.,	K,	Delta
Fisher, Joshua,	E,	Concordia
Goodlander, J. W.,	F,	Clay Center
Griffy, H.,	F,	Hope
Graham, F. M.,	K,	Valley Falls
Graham, H. R.,	E,	Smith Center
Garnet, J. C., s,	A,	Perth
Hale, J. T., capt.,	H,	Galena
Harrison, T. W., c,	K,	Ottowa
Herrill, W.,	A,	Wellington
Hervey; J.,	D,	Topeka
Hollingsworth, K. C., c,	G,	Washington
Howell, R.,	H,	Harper
Hummel, J. L., capt,	H,	Pomona
Hurlbut, D. R.,	K,	Farlinville
Jackson, S.,	G,	Independence
Jones, Philip,	K,	Ark's City
Ketchum, J. S., 1st Lt.,		Minneapolis
Lay, C. F.,	A,	Louisburg
Lacy, J.,	A,	Topeka
Leffler, J.,	A,	Lyndon
Lock, W. M., s,	F,	Newton
Londybarger, J.,	H,	McCune
Mabbett, T.,	D,	Waveland
Martin, Jacob, s,	B,	Girard
Martin, B. M.,	C,	Le Roy
Madden, T.,	G,	Florence
Mather, W. W., Lt.	II,	Topeka
Miller, D. D , c,	A,	Atchison
Mills, B ,	H,	Cheyenne
Moore, W. H.,	C,	Winfield
McAhan, F. M., c,	G,	Fontana
McNew, J. H.,	E,	Hutchinson
McVicker, J.,	F,	Altamont
Nation, Seth.,	A,	Urbana
Newbold, S.,	A,	Neal
Nichols, W. H.,	F,	Empire City
Osborne Jacob,	B,	Meriden
Pearce, J. R.,	E,	Wellington
Puderbaugh, J. M.,	I,	Osawkee
Raber Henry, s,	I,	Haddam
Reynolds D. T.,	A,	Ophir
Richardson, J.,	A,	Lebo
Rigdon, J. W., Lt.,	A,	N. Topeka
Rigdon R. W.,	A,	Silver Lake
Rodgers W., c,	H,	Finney
Foot J. c.	I.	Elk Falls
Rowe, Gab'l,	C,	Ark's City
Salors, Jacob,	K,	Galesburg
Scott, W. F.,	H,	Wichita
Scott, O	B,	Burlington
Sproul Simon,	A,	Harvey
Smith H D., capt.,	D,	Geuda Springs
Smith, P., Lt.,	B,	Kansas City, Mo
Stonebraker, A., s,	E,	Topsy
Thompson, E.,	B,	Lebanon
Tutt, A. J.,	F,	LaCygne
Tyler. W. J ,	F,	Jingo
Tyner, E. H.,	B,	Tannehill
Tyner, M., c,	I,	Michigan Valley
Underwood. J. A.,	B,	Allegan
Van Buskirk, R.,	D.	Mapleton
Walden. A. G.,	K,	Wichita
Whitecotton, A., s,	K,	Wichita
Whiteside, G.,	F,	Topeka
Wimmer, W.,	F,	Hardilee
Windons, P.,	E,	Ellsworth
Wolfe, J. H.,	F,	Wellington

NINTH INFANTRY, 3 MONTHS, 3 YEARS AND
VETERANS.

Cols. R. H. Milroy, G. C. Moody, W. H.
Blake, I. C. B. Suman.

Adams, J. B.,	E,	Roxbury
Allsted, M. L.,	K,	Lawrence
Bailey, A. L., lt.,	B,	Harlan
Baker, J. M.,	G,	Fairmount
Bales, N. W.,	B,	Washington
Baldwin, C., s.,	D,	Hymer
Barnes, J. S.,	D,	Galena
Beiber, C., c	E,	Norton
Bell, A.,	C,	Willow Springs
Boyle, J. G.,	A,	Eureka
Brown, J. W., lt.,	II,	Ness City
Brown, J.,	D,	Yates Center
Bryant, D. L.,	H,	Elk City
Burns, V. O,,	K,	Purity
Burr, L. F.,	A,	Cottonwood Falls
Butts, S. G.,	C,	Mulvane
Byland, S.,	H,	Columbus
Caldwell, L.,	E,	Omio
Carter, I.,	E,	Leavenworth
Clarke, S. R.,	B,	Belmont
Colgrove, H. P.,	C,	Kansas Center
Cramer, B.,	D,	Leavenworth
Cramer, J., capt	B,	Moline
Cutshall, A. H,	B,	Caldwell
De Arment, G.,	E.	Paola
Dilley, A. G., s	H,	Grenola
Doering, A., s	H,	Clifton
Drake, A.,	G,	Parsons
Edson, John, c	II,	Mound Valley
Franklin, R. B., s	I,	Auburn
Fresher, R. R.,	G,	Palatine
Fox, J., s	A,	Elm Creek
Funderberg, P.,	C,	Pittsburg
Garner, M. II.,	C,	Hayesville
Gray, N. K.,	II,	Newbern
Hall, H., s	C,	Sabetha
Haskell, C. F.,	G,	Parsons
Hawkins, T. D.,	II,	Christian
Hinkle, W. H.,	G,	Greensburg
Hudson, W.,	I;	Phillipsburg
Ijams, T. H., capt	K	Garnett
James, H. G..	G	Pittsburg
Kelso, H. S.,	I	Leona
Kendall, J. M.,	A	Lena Valley
Kerlin, M.,	K	Silver Lake
Kelley, M. J.,	A	Washington
Ketchum, C.,	B	Range
Kingsbury, G. N., s	E	Norton
Koplin, J., s	F	Canton
Korn, C. R.,	B	Topeka
Leavitt, G. P., c	E	Paola
Lecklides, S.,	G	Kingman
Lewis, C. N.,		Morganville
Lewis, Eli,	II	Greenleaf
Loomis, N. F.,	C	Galena
Londerback, J. D.,	K	Cecil
Mahaffey, J., lt	I	Beloit
Matthew, R. P..	H	Sterling
McCreery, A. O.,	G	Wetmore
McHenry, J. W..	E	Cuba
Merrifield, W., lt	I	Abilene
Miller, Isaiah, c	K	Burlington
Miller, G. W.,	I	Traer
Milner, G. N.,	H	Chester, Neb
Morgan, W. J., s	G	Kingman
Morgan, W. H., m		Peabody
Morris, S. J.,	C	Marietta
Morrison, H. J.,	H	Garnett
Nafus, J. H,,	F	Erie

Name	Co.	Place
Nodurfth, J. H., c	I	Cherryvale
Oliver, J. J.,	I	Wichita
Parker, G. W., c	E	Fredonia
Parks, H.,	I	Bonita
Pedrick, S.,	C	Leavenworth
Pritchard, J. T.,	G	Marshall
Pritchard, T,,	G	Greensburg
Proctor, D.,	I	Concordia
Record, W. L.,	C	Beloit
Rees, J.,	C	Ellinwood
Reese, G.,		Sorghum
Reilly, J.,	B	Ellinwood
Rickets, J.,	D	Chanute
Ronster, F..	C	Ellinwood
Sherwood, Jas.,	E	Minersville
Shigley, W.,	D	Humboldt
Shrock, E. W., c	C	Newton
Smith, H.,	C	Carbondale
Smith, H.,	C	Iola
Stebbins, S. B., s	I	Cecil
Stiles, A.,	A	Burns
Strombaugh, A.,	K	Hartford
Sutton, W. F.,	B	Keightly
Tarbell, W. I.,	I	Corbett
Thornton, R.,	F	New Albany
Thornton, J. H.,	G	Sedgewick
Tibbitts, J.,	G	Raceburg
Timmons, S. G.,	G	Fredonia
Tobias, W. P.,		Riley Center
Todd, W. H.,	C	Pleasant Green
Wallis, J.,	C	Morantown
White, J. L.,	G	Middleton
Weeks, S. B., s		Phillipsburg
White, C.,	B	Oswego
Wolf, J.,	C	Defiance
Wood, L. M., lt	K	Clifton
Young, C. H.,	A	Rawlins

TENTH INFANTRY, 3 MONTHS, AND THREE YEARS.

Cols. M. D. Manson, W. C. Kise, W. B. Carroll, Marsh B. Taylor.

Name	Co.	Place
Allen, T. W.,	B	Neosho Falls
Alton, M. F.,	B	Little River
Anderson, A.,	C	Council Grove
Anderson, J. W.,	A	Kirwin
Asbel, C. H.,	E	Marion
Bate, C. H.,	C	Sedgewick
Bates, C.,	A	Independence
Bechtol, J. G.,	G	Everest
Browning, S. R.,	H	Chanute
Bennett, M.,	F	Elk Falls
Berry, H..	A	Girard
Bicking, A. T.,	I	Ft Scott
Booker, A.,	C	Castleton
Boyle, H. A.,	I	Wellington
Bunyan, A. W.,	D	McPherson
Cheney, H. A.,c	G	New Tabor
Cooley, W. F.,	A	Waco
Cox, J..	K	Litchfield
Creek, C.,	D	Pontiac
De Spain, J. H., c	B	Council Grove
Doty, C.,	G	Cherryvale
Downing, H. P.,		Rosalia
Dougherty, S. L., s	I	Red Bud
Downing, A. B.,	D	Little River
Elston, A.,	H	Hays City
Essex, J.,	F	Burlington
Ethington, S. S.,	B	Chalk Mound
Finley, W., c	I	Atwood
Forgey, J. S.,	B	Wellsville
Gallaher, L.,	C	Cherryvale
Grimes, R. R., c	F	Severy

Name	Co.	Residence
Hamilton, A.,	I	Marion
Hamilton, J. H., capt	A	Downs
Hamlin, D.,		Ft. Scott
Hill, C. W.,	G	Parsons
Hollingsworth, D.,	F	Elk Falls
Hunt, T.,	B	Baldwin
James, J. A., bugler,	E	N. Topeka
Jennings, R. L.,	D	McPherson
Jones, T. A., s	G	Toronto
Keller, S. M.,	C	Lenora
Kempton, D.,	I	Burden
La Rue, A	A	Columbus
Laugh, W., bugler,	K	Douglass
Laybourn, W.,		La Mont's Hill
Lipp, S. W., c	K	Sedgewick City
Litchfield, J.,	I	Oswego
Lowder, D., s	C	Beloit
Manker, L.,	B	Topeka
Mason, W. B.,	D	Parsons
Mare, W. A.,	C	Howard
Martin, J. F.,	K	Osage City
Marks, L. H.,	F	Osborne
Martin, J. P,,	B	Lane
Maxson, M., c	A	Peru
McCowan, W. H.,	H	Coffeyville
McKensie, J.,	A	Baxter Springs
McLaughlin, O. F., m	C	Paola
Miller, G.,	D	Leavenworth
Miller, J. S., lt	H	Wichita
Moon, W. W.,	A	Cherryvale
Morgan, W. T.,	B	Paola
Norris, C. W., c	A	Cherryvale
Osborne, J. W. C.,	A	Cherryvale
Painter, W. B., s	F	Lawrence
Payne, M.,	E	Nickerson
Peterson, S.,	B	Junction City
Pock, J. A.,	F	Oak Valley
Riley, S.,	K	Amboy
Scott, L. H.,	H	Burlington
Shepard, F. M.,	A	Denmark
Simler, H.,	E	Topeka
Simmons, S. M.,	D	Caldwell
Slade, E. B., s	G	Lecompton
Smith, G. H.,	H	Saronburg
Snyder, J. M.,	D	Downs
Spike, J., c	D	Caldwell
Spillman, J.,	C	Monmouth
Spencer, C.,	C	Paola
Snyder, H.,	E	Topeka
St. Clair, A.,	F	Reagle
Tanquary. L. S., c	C	Columbus
Truit, James B.,	G	Waverly
Underhill, J. A.,	G	Conway Springs
Voorhees, D.,	D	Bitlertown
Ward, T. K.,	F	Adrian
Watson, W., s	C	Osborne
West, R. R., s	I	Chelsea
White, W.,	B	Greenleaf
Young, H.,	D	Greenwich

ELEVENTH INFANTRY ZOUAVES, 3 YEARS, 3 MONTHS AND VETERANS.

Cols. L. Wallace. G. F. McGinnis and Dan McCauley.

Name	Co.	Residence
Alexander, T. P., lt	I	Florence
Bailey, W. H.,	H	Topeka
Baird, J. R.,	I	Spearville
Ball, H.,	E	Edmonds
Barrett, J. A.,	G	Wellsville
Belzer, H.,	K	Burns
Banon, F., c	C	Douglass
Bennett, S.,	G	Burr Oak
Berg, W..	B	Crestline
Beymer, J. G., s	B	Florence

Name	Co.	Place
Bodkin, H. C.,	H	Neosho Rapids
Bowers, J. M.,	K	Topeka, Pauline
Britton, D. D.,	D	Ozark
Britton, A. H., s	E	Section
Brothers, H. E.,	B	Hamilton
Brown, F. G.,	G	Hutchinson
Brown, S. W.,	I	Keystone
Buckingham, J.,	B	Oskaloosa
Carter, S. P.,	H	Emporia
Carter, J. R.,	H	Wellington
Chambers, J. H.,	B	Howard
Charles, W. S.,	B	N. Topeka
Cleland, W. H.,	F	Hoyt
Coffman, E. C.,	G	Pottersburg
Cook, J. B.,	G	Keamsville
Cook, J. L., s	G	Gove City
Cook, H.,	I	Kingman
Cossand, R. H., c	G	Caldwell
Cottman, J. D.,	C	Oxford
Crawford, J. T.,	A	Parsons
Critchfield, J. N., s	K	Arkansas City
Currart, T.,	B	Howard
Curtis, W. H.,	I	N. Topeka
Dailey, A. D.,	D	Neodesha
Darnall, W. W., lt col		Ft Scott
Downing, D. J.,	F	Millerton
Duley, C. H.,	A	Lawrence
Dunbar, W. C.,	B	Fall River
Duncan, I. P.,	K	Humboldt
Durham T W, lt	G	Topeka
Durham, C. J., fife major,		Douglass
Dumont, J. F.,	A	Topeka
Elliot, W. P.,	I	Marsh
Emanuel, G.,	C	Lyons
Eyestone, G. W.	E	Caldwell
Fielding, R.,	F	Matanzas
Gebhart, W. A.,	B	Topeka
Gharst, E.,	C	Xenia
Gibson, W. C.	A	Salina
Godfrey, J. D.,	B	Towanda
Goodwin, J.,	E	Burrton
Gregg, A. H.,	G	Leanna
Griffith, D. G.	B	Independence
Hall, J.,	H	Matfield Green
Hallowell, J. R.,	C	Wichita
Hammon, T.,	C	Scandia
Hanna, J. T.,	G	Topeka
Hicks, J. S.,	C	Abilene
Hilbert, S.,	C	Grenola
Hill, J. H., s	G	Sterling
Hinton, H.,	A	Logan
Hodge, L. D.,	B	Sterling
Hogue, J. H,	B	Montana.
Hoover, J. W.,	H	Abilene
Hottle, B. F.,	G	Field
Holloway, M. J.,	E	Greenleaf
Howe, Henry W.,	A	Lawrence
Hundredmark, H.,	H	Lincoln
Joseph, A. C.,	K	Topeka
Johnson, J. H., s	B	Irving
King, J. M.,	H	Independence
King, J. D.,	I	Wyandotte
Knetzer, C. B.,	D	Eric
Knight, W. W.,	A	Hartford
Ladd, W. D, s	C	Douglas
Kafferty, W. L.,	G	Fredonia
Laramore, T., c	B	Winfield
Lesley, Simon,	G	Cloverdale
Lawhead, F.,	A	Sterling
Lewis, W.	G	Coyville
Lewis, J. T.,	G	Cherokee
Loper, I.,	F	Pomona
Lorry, F.,	E	Arkansas City
Long, S., s	F	Xenia

Name	Co.	Place
Lynn, C. W.,	A	Leon
Mapes, J. B., c	A	Fort Scott
Marks, I.,	I	Oswego
Martin, W. L.,	D	Winfield
LcClure, J. M.,	I	Milan
McCall, J. H.'	G	Topeka
McKinzie, J. A.,	F	Eldorado
McLaughlin, J. A., lt	K	Topeka
Mikesell, J.	I	Sedan
Miller, H. H.,	C	Irving
Miller, J. R., c	H	Ellenwood
Modiset, J. F.,	C	Fredonia
Mudbarger, G. W.	E	Topeka
Muse, B.,	I	Parsons
Musgrave, J.,	B	La Harp
Musser, B. B.,		Parsons
Napier, J. H.,	D	Eldorado
Newton, B. B.,	F	Bashan
Nye, J. C.,	D	Detroit
Osborne, J. O.,	H	Garnett
Osborne, R., c	E	Fort Scott
Oslter, J.,	F	St. John or Sterling
Painter, G.,	A	Mommouth
Poole, W.,	C	Peoria
Price, E. J.,	C	New Albany
Ray, S. W.	E	South Cedar
Rice, A.,	C	Lerado
Richards, J. J.,	A	New Albany
Richardson, R.,	B	Independence
Ripley, W.,	C	Havana
Rockwell, W., surg.,		Rockwell City
Rohm, G. W.,	H	Newbern
Schardine, J.,	C	Nickerton
Schlusser, W.,	B	Augusta
Shannon, J. H.	B	Girard
Shepley, D. V.,	B	Oswego
Sims, J. R.,	G	Emporia
Stahl, J.,	I	Earlton
Steele. J. C.,	C	Howard
Steinmire, C. H.,	F	Seneca
Sturdevant, C. N., C.	A	Larned
Strohm, L.,	I	Ft. Scott
Slaven. S.,	B	Milan
Taylor. I.. V. B.,	E	Frankfort
Tayne, W.,	C	Americus
Uselman, A. S.,	D	Prescott
Vandergrift, M., c,	K	Leavenworth
Veach, S. B , c,	B	Parsons
Vogue, F.,	H	Chelsea
Warbriton, J., sgt.,	G	Garnett
Watson. F. M.,	C	Mulvane
Watts, W. A.,	F	Elsinore
Welch, C. M., s,	E	Topeka
Wells, E. T.,	I	Neodasha
West, W. T., c,	E	Ft. Scott
Wheeler, S.,		Iola
Wise, A. J.,	I	N. Topeka
Wood, A.,	D	Humboldt

TWELFTH INFANTRY, 1 YEAR AND 3 YEARS.

Cols. J. M. Wallace, Wm. H. Link and R. Williams.

Name	Co.	Place
Adams, M. L.,	F	Cawker City
Alexander, J. M.,	F	Oxford
Baker, D.,	H	Minneapolis
Barnes, J. E.,	I	Clyde
Barney, D. C. M.,	G	Elk City
Bayliff, W. D.,	E	Emporia
Bennett, W. M.,	G	Cherryvale
Bibler, S.,	I	Dexter City
Bickham, P. D.,	B	Altamont
Blander, W.,	H	Ozark
Blowers, G. M.,	B	Beloit
Boicourt, J. C., s,	H	Easton
Bolton, B. E.,	F	Howard

Name		Place
Bradley, L.,	B	Jamestown
Brandon, H., surg.,		Wichita
Bundrum, C., o s,	B	Arkansas City
Burris, J. C.,	B	Verdigris
Cartmell, J. H., c,	D	Mound City
Case, C. H.,	I	Havensville
Cawhill, G. W.,	B	Cherryvale
Chalmers, G.,	C	Burlington
Clark, S. W.,		Minneapolis
Coil, Uriah, s,	E	Lincoln
Copper, N.,	G	Cherokee
Cox, E. H., s,	C	Belmont
Davis, J. S.,	D	Lowe
Davis, W.,	K	LaCygne
Dentzer, G. H.,	E	Abilene
Dafrom, G. M.,	D	Plum Grove
Druley, S. E.,	C	Peru
Elder, J. M.,	D	Monroe
Ellis, W. H. 1st s,	C	New Lancaster
Elwood, D. R.,	C	Douglas
Farley, T. P., s,	D	Valley Falls
Flickinger, J.,	I	Winfield
Fleaner, J ,	C	Sunnydale
Frank, C.,	I	Great Bend
Graves, H. H., lt,	K	Kingman
Green, D. A.,	H	Bunker Hill
Gemmer, P.,	H	Waterloo
Hall, I.,	K	Barton
Hickman, A. J., s,	H	Liberty
House, J. A,,	H	Silver Lake
Hubbard, J.,	A	Roy
Ireland, W., s	D	Lawrence
Jaslin, G. W.,	B	Tower Springs
Jones, E.,	E	Fredonia
King, J. F,,	A	Garnett
Klotz, A.,	C	Wilson
Kulp, D. H , c	E	Fact
Laswell, E. J.,	C	Augusta
LenFresty, E. S., capt	C	Topeka
Little, J. G.,	A	Veitsburg
Lock, H.,	K	Topeka
Longoor, A. J.,	I	Osage Mission
Mather, A. J.,	I	Hollensburg
McCann, T. J.,	C	Springdale
McLaughlin, T. J.,	K	N. Topeka
Miner, E. W.,	B	Axtell
Moore, W. H.,	F	Hays City
Mitchell, C	A	LaCygne
Morlan, D. C.,	D	Eskridge
Naughton, M.,	A	Medicine Lodge
Neal, J. W.,	D	Wichita
Nelson, N.,	I	Melvern
Newby, W. S.,	D	Sedgewick
Peters, H.,	G	Yates Center
Phillips, M.,	G	Otto
Preston, L. Y.,	B	Scottsville
Rhodes, G.W.,	I	Wauneta
Roof, J. A.,	F	Chilicothe, Mo
Riley. A. F.,	B	Lynn
Rogerson, P.,	B	Oak Hill
Sanders, C.,	G	Milo
Scott, C.,	I	Medicine Lodge
Smith, E. M.,	F	Paola
Smith, W. H.,	F	Paola
Smith, A. H.,	D	Wauneta
Snodgrass, J. M.,	E	Kenneth
Southerly, E.,	E	Oswego
Swarrow, W. H., lt	I	Parsons
Spence, S. A., m		Clay Center
Stanton, E.,	F	Topeka
Stewart, J. W.,	A	Glen Grouse
Steel, T., c	G	Oakwood
Swartz, E.,	C	Eldorado
Thompson, J., m		Clay Center

Name	Co.	Place
Thurston, T. J., s	I	Alton
Tobias, N.,	A	Manhattan
Vail E H	E	Chanute
Vest J T c	K	Clay Center
Weed J	G	Burlington
Wendell W A	B	Arkansas City
White R	F	Rosetta
Whittem Q A	K	Iola
Williams D E lt	A	Carlyle
Winters A A	E	Altoona
Wright S J	B	Fellsburg
Wright J F	A	Vermilion
Wyand I c	D	Severy

THIRTEENTH INFANTRY, THREE YEARS AND VETERAN.

Cols. J. C. Sullivan, R. S. Foster, C. J. Dobbs.

Name	Co.	Place
Alley E A	K	Oskaloosa
Alpha J M	D	Anthony
Anderson S J	A	Arkansas City
Bennett M T	K	Burden
Bland R H s	I	Delhi
Boonewell L K s	G	Winfield
Bowen A C	D	Sylvan Grove
Boyer M	I	Cedarville
Branderburg J W	F	Joppa
Brown John	I	Omio
Case R	E	Victor
Coffee W H	G	Parsons
Crable J	I	Wichita
Crist A	F	Eden Valley
Davis J H	A	Augusta
Dolsby M	K	America City
Dure Steavers	B	Meriden
Francis J K lt	I	Wichita
Froment W	E	Belle Plaine
Glace J A	I	Carter Creek
Gordouier H F	A	Newton
Graham R	I	Newton
Graham R J major		Newton
Green W S	C	Baxter Springs
Harden J B c	H	Dexter
Hamilton J W	G	Guelph
Hedrick G	G	Columbus
Herrod M	E	Tisdale
Hiler A	A	Burr Oak
Holder W	C	Montana
Johnson J c	I	Valley Center
Jones F M	B	Cato
Luckwood J	D	Neodesha
Mahan W J s	G	Baxter Springs
Miller J R	E	Torrance
Miller G W	D	Salina
Mitchel Chas	A	La Cygne
McKee J G	I	Glasco
Mounts J H	F	Winfield
Perkins B F	A	Osage City
Robinson D P	E	South Haven
Ruhel J E s	I	Rush Center
Seward J C c	E	Sterling
Skinner W H s	A	Ness City
Snead H M	K	Salina
Smith W L c	E	Lyons
Smith C O	B	Harbin Neb
Smith C	E	Morantown
Skydgel J	E	Mantanzas
Spencer C	E	McCune
Stone J E	A	Topeka
Strong E	K	Rosalia
Styles M	B	Sterling
Surran C	G	Torry
Talcott H Wm		Iola
Trueblood A C capt	G	Atchison

Vanderpool J M	F	Cloverdale
Van Pelt	H	Oberlin
Wedenberger G B	E	Waterville
Wood J L	E	Topeka
Woolf S W	F	Atchison

FOURTEENTH INFANTRY THREE YEARS.

Col's N Kimball, Wm Harrow and John Coons.

Anderson R N	s	K	Constant
Baumgartel O		K	Cave Springs
Coleman S S		H	Fall River
Dailey J A		E	Topeka
Davis W W		C	Winfield
Dowdell J S	c	I	N Topeka
Edwards J W		F	Newton
Farleigh L		H	Grenola
Foster A W		G	Alden
Gaw J W		I	Galena
Hall E N		C	Harper
Harrel J M	c	D	Iuka
Hogue J C		K	Edmond
Hooker E H		I	Barnesville
Hoffman W	s	B	Newton
Hudson T	s	A	Independence
Johnson C M		B	Dunlap
Johnson J H		H	Kelso
Kelley W R	s	D	Opolis
King W		H	Junction City
Knapp G W band m			Douglas
Land A		H	Ridgeway
Lease J		H	Hiawatha
Logan D W		F	Raymond
Markle H G	m		New Albany
Mayfield J	m	A	Jonesburg
McCoy M	c	C	Cleveland
McMillan J A		A	Wichita
Miller H		I	Eureka
Morgan E J	s	A	Crestline
Morgan J S		F	Brookville
Maris E		A	Eldorado
Newbank C E		E	Bel·it
Olmstead W		I	Udall
O'Donald B		D	Fowler
Pauley J J		A	East Wolf
Payne T G	s	I	Larned
Phillips C		I	Augusta
Pierson W P		H	Thayer
Roe Ezra	s	V R C	Concordia
Rush Jos		I	Otto
Sherran N W		B	Eldorado
Spainbower G W		H	Coffeyville or Dora
Stafford M		C	Peru
Thayer C C		D	Clifford
Wellborn J W		H	Kingman
White J		I	Topeka
White J		I	Roxbury
Wills J		D	Lyndon
Wilson M D		H	Caldwell
Winans J M		H	Newton or Attica

FIFTEENTH INFANTRY, THREE YEARS.

Cols. G. D. Wagner, G. A. Wood.

Banks G L	s	C	Coffeyville
Barkhurst C W		D	Columbus
Beaver A		D	Center Ridge
Birchfield J Q		K	Howard
Brady T		E	Schell City Mo
Burcham H D		E	Bone Springs
Chatfield W		C	Mound Valley
Conover F		I	El Dorado
Crew C P		E	Nal'l Mil Home
Crane L C		A	New Lancaster
Davenport A		D	Fall River

Davis W S	B	Colony
DuBois J A s	I	Anthony
Dusenbury G W	D	Mullinsville
Edenburn P	A	Lincoln
Edwards E A	K	Topeka
Ewing A C	K	Vallonia
Fowler A capt & maj B		Uniontown
Goldsmith J L	K	Cecil
Goodyear L	C	Marvin
Graham T lt	G	Lawrence
Green A	B	Coffeyville
Greenburg N E	A	Colfax
Hamilton J W	A	Topeka
Hardesty G D	H	Hardillie
Henning J F c	K	Emporia
Hickok F M	K	Kansas City
Jay H C	B	Baldwin
Lemphree Silas	G	Nat'l Mil Home
Macy J D	I	Sterling
Maxson O N	D	Bennington
Maxwell A F	G	Americus
Miller J B wagoner	K	Neosho Falls
Miller Geo	C	Leavenworth
Milliken N s	B	Topeka
Mitchel J	D	Fulton
Mitchel W R c	F	Elgin
Mitchel C R drummer	A	Geuda Springs
Mouras M	A	Rock Cowley Co
Neal W	E	Girard
Peed J	F	Mona
Plumb G c	H	Hayesville
Powers W F	H	Greensburgh
Rawlins G	F	Pomona
Salron N J c	I	Walnut
Scott A H	K	Geneva
Sheldon L	G	N Topeka
Smith Ferd	B	Wilson
Smith T L	H	Tonganoxie
Smith John		Rochester
Smith J H capt	G	Columbus
Snodgrass G W c	D	Little River
Swords J	A	Columbus
Taylor D C	H	Kingman
Thompson J N	A	Parsons
Truett C H	K	Waverly
Tullis W H s	K	Girard
Wade D F	F	Neodesha
Walker J W	E	Turon
Weaver R S lt	G	Holton
Wilson J M	C	Wichita
Wright W H	F	Osage Mission
Wolever J	G	Fredonia
Vaughn Ob	C	Tecumseh
Whitehead J M chaplain		Silver Lake

SIXTEENTH INFANTRY ONE YEAR,
Col's P. A. Hackleman and T. J. Lucas.

SIXTEENTH INFANTRY THREE YEARS.
Col's T. J. Lucas and R. Conover.

Allen J M lieut.	I	Urbana
Barr W N	B	Clifton
Beck M M c	K	Holton
Bell M	I	Hamilton
Biddell A J	K	Valencia
Briggs R	D	Coffeyville
Busby R F	C	Busby
Campbell A B c	E	Topeka
Carter J	D	Waterloo
Chenoweth W E capt I		Arkansas City
Chilty J B	A	Abilene
Clark F	B	Burlington
Cookson E	A	Winfield
Copeland W lt	I	Winfield

Name	Co.	Place
Corteny T c	E	Bennes
Criswell D s	I	Damorris
Cogswell J P	F	Carbondale
Connell W A c	I	Wyandotte
Davis J C	E	Wichita
Day N H	I	Leonardville
Dimick A c	E	Eureka
Edmundson J M	G	Ottawa
Edwards T J	K	Altoona
Ellis E	H	Cicero
Fender G W	K	Topeka
Fields T	G	Gibson
Fisher W L	E	Centralia
Fisk R S	F	Altoona
Fitty C	D	McLouth
Fleming M H	B	Ottawa
Gilfillan D G	D	Independence
Garlick S B	I	Atchison
Gard J F	B	Cherryvale
Gottschack L	I	Pearlette
Gordon H	B	Hutchison or Mona
Greadzner L	E	Atchison
Hailesfall G W	F	Netawaka
Hamilton J	C	Jamestown
Harrison T J c	D	Auburn
Harrison T J c	D	Topeka
Howka C A	I	Urbana
Hawklns L J s	F	Chanute
Howell G W	H	Farlington
Hudson W D	D	Girard
Keener W H	A	Grover
Langman J	A	Roy
Laymon J	A	Alta
Lockwood J	H	Neodesha
Losey W T	K	Millerton
Mackliu J E capt	K	Ft. Leavenworth
Medsker J L	I	Fort Scott
McCartny H A	F	St. Marys
Moore Thos. c	C	Doster
Morgan A W		Lawrence
Oldham Z	K	Winfield
Paggett W F	C	Wa -Keeney
Paris J M	I	Cimarron
Parsons R M	D	Cawker City
Pearson J	G	Harper
Pendergrast C H	D	Abilene
Perrine R M	D	Cawker City
Potts N J ·	D	Cawker City
Powell J M	A	Quaker Vale
Reed R s		Abilene
Rose J A	C	Wellington
Russell	C	Rantoul
Scott J A	K	South Cedar
Slade C P lt	K	Rossville
Starbuck H C	B	Florence
St. Clair W H	B	Long Island
Talbott T F	I	Urbana
Tibbetts O T	E	Bonita
Trester A	D	Wellington
Trew S T	H	Cleveland
Tull S lt	H	Burden
Walker L	G	Plymoth
Walters S	H	Altamont
Walters M VB	H	Altamont
Weaver H C	H	Winfield
Weston W H capt	B	Cherryvale
Whistle J H	E	Eldorado
Wilkey J M	C	Independence
Wyatt O W	F	Garnett
Ward R G s	B	Sedan

SEVENTEENTH INFANTRY MOUNTED, THREE YEARS AND VETFRAN,

Cols. M. S. Hascall, J. T. Wilder, J. G. Vail.

Allison W	K	Willis
Anderson H T	I	Ellsworth
Barrett N N m	H	Fredonia
Barrett J J m	H	Fredonia
Barnes W R c	I	Mound Valley
Bass J W		Ft Scott
Blue E	D	Abilene
Bennett R M	I	Liberty
Booth J G	I	Waco or Mulvane
Bright J	F	Kiowa
Brown H D	D	Hampton
Bruner C G	D	Carlyle
Burns G W	C	Kiowa
Chestnut F J	H	Clay Center
Clifford C G	D	Shady Bend
Clifford E W lt	G	Osage City
Connett W		Haven
Coulson W F s	B	Anthony
Crosby J	I	Sutphens Mill
Daughters S	I	Rosalia
Deans R	B	Concordia
Dilworth C	I	Guelph
Doubleday J	B	Caldwell
English S	E	Peabody
Fisher J lt	K	Eldorado
Foust S J	E	Baltimore
Funk H	C	Strawn
Godfrey A J s	B	Burr Oak
Godfrey D H	B	Burr Oak
Hamilton J R	B	Norton
Hamlin W	H	Strawn
Hauenstein J	K	Elk Falls
Harrison J A	A	Sandago
Hayden G F capt	F	Hutchinson
Hough H D	I	Brazilton
Hedgelin T H	H	Long Island
Hardin A	A	Eldorado
Hinch H C	E	Cecil
Hite J T s	G	Arkansas City
Hodge C W	I	Sterling
Hoffman W	B	Pleasant View
Hoffman H K	B	Fulton
Hogan A J	K	Elk Falls
Howey J Q		Parsons
Hubbard J J	C	Oxford
Hubbard A J	K	Elk Falls
Hunt J F c	F	Baxter Springs
Jackson M A	E	Lincoln
Jones J L capt	K	Cecil
Judd R	H	Osage Mission
Kautz D	F	Cedar Vale
Keeler J G	F	Oneida
Kiler J	E	Columbus
Lacey J	K	Lawrence
LaForce J B	F	Cecil
McClure R M	H	Mound City
McKenzie S	B	Columbus
McAdams W	C	Buffalo
McKinney J G c	G	Paola
McMahan J	C	Oxford
Mellville F s	A	Howard
Metzger J S	B	Minneapolis
Miller J S	B	Millerton
Moore H	E	Bloomfield
Myers Z B	I	Winfield
Ober J	G	Garnett
Orton J	G	Barnard
O'Neal J H m	C	Warrensburg
Paddock H	F	Grainfield
Parker W A	K	Wyandotte

Parr E T	D	Hampton
Plummer J E	E	Chanute
Poff J A	E	Lawrence
Proctor J N	G	Springside
Pough I	H	Hiattville
Roebuck T I	A	Elk City
Shoemaker J B	F	Altamont
Showan D P	C	Ft. Scott
Smith J A	A	Ottawa
Smith Geo R	I	Butler Mo
Tillbury W M	F	Lotta
Vail J G col		Leavenworth
Voris W S	D	Arkansas City
Ward J W	A	Salem
Watson B	I	Mulvane
Withers S K s		Topeka
Wootan V A s		Cherokee

EIGHTEENTH INFANTRY, 3 YEARS AND VET-
ERAN.

Col's Thos. Pattison, H. D. Washburn,
D. R. Bowden.

Adair T J	A	Newton
Aikman R	C	Ft. Scott
Alexander N	C	Paola
Art W T		Arkansas City
Bailey G W lt	A	Wichita
Baker Cha's	H	Wabaunsee
Barker C c		Wabaunsee
Brown S Clay surg		Topeka
Burks J H		Hartford
Coble Dan		Concordia
Cornell J H	D	Burdgeville
Dickman C W	D	Sedan
Eastman L W m		Spearville
Haskell M M	C	Bodock
Hendricks M	I	Howard
Higbie A S	C	Ft Scott
Johnson H	A	Baldwin
Jones J H	G	Farlington
Keith J W	D	Dodge City
Kingman J P	E	Argentine
Lewis O		Newton
Lee W R adjt & c s		Lyons
McCabe J		Girard
McCaslin J c		Chanute
Morrow R C		Lapland
Richerdson T E m		Ellsworth
Roberts, J s	G	Sarenburg
Ross J F lt	F	Sylvan Grove
Sherman A C	E	Rossville
Speer S M	F	Wichita
Stevenson R W	K	Whitfield
Story R C c	I	Atchison
Strain F s	G	Phillipsburg
Scroggins J C'		La Cygne
Tuttle A C	C	Nickerson
Thornton W	A	Kansas City, Ks
Wantland B J	B	Eureka
Washburn C K	I	Caldwell
Weston J	G	Cherryvale
Williams Jud	A	Ottawa
Williams J K	B	Florence
Weston W H	G	Cherryvale
Yager J L c	K	Columbus

NINETEENTH INFANTRY, THREE YEARS AND
VETERAN.

Cols. Sol Meredith, S. J. Williams, J. M.
Lindley.

Adams James c	G	Abilene
Archer Wm	E	Peabody
Bales E H	K	Andover
Bales J L	K	Wichita

Barnes J M	I	Mid valle
Beagle W A	E	Cherryvale
Barnett T chaplain		Ft Scott
Beemont	G	Argentine
Blackledge H c	C	Sterling
Brahan J N	D	Topeka
Bradbury J	B	Arkansas City
Castater W H	B	Sedgwick or Wichita
Cline S	A	Independence
Coady W H	H	Long Island
Cochran P	E	Cold Springs
Collins N	F	Eldorado
Crabtree A R	D	Burns
Craig E A	C	Chetopa
Crowell J W (fife maj)	C	Harts Mills
Ellison J B	A	South Haven
Eacret W H	E	Buffalo
Gillett J W P H	C	Castleton
Hiatt J P	C	Fall River
Hawk D	K	Topsy
Harter D G	K	Tower Springs
Heath R W	E	Wellington
Helvic J s	K	Muscotah
Holden L R	F	Osage Mission
Hubble John	I	Chetopa
Hufford G W	E	Dragoon
Hindman S lt	B	Topeka
Ingraham M	G	Norway
Jackson R	K	Tower Springs
Leonard F B	.I	Sedan
Leonard F C	I	Wauneta
McDonald H	H	Leonardsville
McGregor J	A	Litchfield
McRoberts C L	D	Winfield
Ogg F R	I	Olathe
Pearson J e	A	South Haven
Phillips C W s		Tonganoxie
Pickell D	A	Alma
Pugh H D	I	Halstead
Rathbun G M	C	Sedan
Rathbun J R c	C	Sedan
Rich Eli	C	Parsons
Russey J M adjt		Pittsburg
Sarr H	E	Coyville
Shockley J	E	Delmore
Sholty W M	K	Hooversville
Short W capt	H	Fredona
Small W P	D	Veitsburg
Smith F M	H	Delhi
Smith W H	G	Burns
Stonebraker A	K	Topsy
Stonebraker S s	K	Topsy
Taylor L V B s	A	Frankfort
Wiley L	I	Chelsea
Winters L D	I	Sigel
Young W	H	Ottawa

TWENTIETH INFANTRY, THREE YEARS AND VETERAN.

Col's W. L. Brown, J. Van Valkenburg, John Wheeler, W. C. L. Taylor, Wm Orr and A. S. Anderson.

Adams J c	C	Rhodes
Antrim T E •	I	Little Valley
Babbitt W H	I	Newton
Barnes W H	G	Prairie Center
Benefiel E	F	Wichita
Bennett J	C	Cherryvale
Bergwood L G	F	Parsons
Bird J W	A	Corinth
Bonebrake J C	F	Oak Valley
Bryan J M	G	Sedan
Bunce Tho's	D	Chase

Name	Co.	Place
Bunce T C	D	Prosper
Burch T C	B	Middleton
Cessna J N e	E	Oswego
Cornan C G s	I	Rock
Cox A I	D	Longton
Craigmiller J	G	Lawrence
Cules S	E	Burns
Curtis G G	B	Gherryvale
Darst A F e	B	Rose
Deibert R M	A	Oskaloosa
Dey R D	G	Pittsburg
Dobbins A	K	New Chilicothe
Doubleday J	D	Caldwell
Drake G	E	Erie
Ferguson J E	G	Delphos
Fix John	D	Grimm
Frasier A	B	Pleasant Run
Gillespie G F	C	Fulton
Gillespie G T	G	Dayton
Grin J	A	Stockton
Hampton J H	G	Parsons
Harter D G s	E	Tower Springs
Hawkins D	D	Parsons
Hazlet J	F	Wichita
Hewitt J W lt	C	Fort Scott
Heustis G F	E	Wabaunsee
Hoffman J	B	Orsborne
Hogue C s	·C	Barnes
Hoover J capt	A	Canton
Hunter J C	G and F	Towando
Jenkius W F	F	Fort Scott
Kirk J C capt	F	Wichita
Loyd G P	B	Sedan
March J	E	Ellsworth
McMillen D	A	Melvern
McPheeters J A M s	K	Rosedalle
Moore Chas	F	Wyandotte
Miller N E lt	H	Oberlin
Morgan M	F	Wamego
Moore J W lt	E	Assaria
Murphy O c	D	Pleasanton
Nelson John	B	Minneapolis
Null S W s	K	Parsons
O'Donald B	B	Fowler
Parker M B	K	Reamsville
Porter W C chaplain		Ft Scott
Raber S	E	Clinton
Rains Milton	A	Densmore
Rains J	A	Edmond
Richardson D	B	Glen Elder
Riggin J W	F	Clifford
Salisbury F M m		Hepler
Scritchfield J H	B	Westmoreland
Shaw I J	F	Otto or Hepler
Sexton J G s	G and F	Fredoria
Savage J E c	D	Richmond
Skinner H	A	Wyandotte
Sanders J T	B	Wellington
Smiley J A	F	Howard
Stephens T W s	K	North Topeka
Strode G W	F	Wichita
Taylor R H capt	F	Tonganoxie
Toliver R c	K	Havensville
Warren G W	B	Hutchinson
Willard J S s	G	Hutchinson
Williams J M	K	Glen Elder

Name	Co.	Location
Baker J	G	Iola
Barcus S A	D	Rest or Fawn Creek
Barkdell W	D	Clyde
Beach J M	D	Cherryvale
Bently E c	I	Marysville
Best T E s	B	Ivy
Bowlen W D	E	Almena
Booker P R	C	McCune
Brann R M	I	Prescott
Brodie W A	D	Chapman
Brothwell D	A	Wakefield
Brown Ed m	K	Yates Center
Burnett H	E	Waterville
Campbell R	I	Cleardale
Card B F lt	L	Emporia
Cart R T	M	Clay Center
Carter J	B	Chelsea
Cartright J	D	Kingman
Cooprider W	I	McPherson
Cooprider J	I	Trenton
Cromwell L H c	I	Atwood
Davis R A	B	Paola
Davis H T b	L	Mulberry Grove
Duncan M V b	K	Columbus or Oswego
Eckard H G s	I	Oxford
Elston J	B	Minneapolis
Evans J M	E	Wilsey
Fisher C	M	Burlingame
Frink A P	A	Oxford
Garrett J H capt	D	Lawrence
Golding T	M	Kansas City Ks
Grubbs J W	F	Burrton
Hall J T	D	South Mound
Hamilton J G	B	Derby
Hancock M	L	Scandia
Harlan H	E	Cherryvale
Haskins C	A	Hayesville
Hendricks I C major		Anthony
Hendricks	I	Globe
Holt J S	H	Sherman City
Houston J A		Clay Genter
Hudson W	E	Liberty
Hutchinson J G	K	Melvern
Jones D S	M	Bavaria
Kauble I	I	Empire City
Kennedy J H	E	Mahone
Kinnerly R F	D	South Mound
Kimball J	F	Chautauqua
Kimball W	F	Sedan
Louderback A	H	Empire City
McClure J S	L	Topeka
McFaddin J C lt	I	St Marys
Mires H S	G	Guelph
Moore J A	H	Newton
Morris A	G	Morantown
Morris J	I	Cedarvale
Murray C	K	Oswego
Noblett F W capt	F	Dora
Norman E	C	Bennington
Olmstead H	A	Ozark
Palmer J W s	E	N Topeka
Pettus J M	B	Dodge City
Pierce D M	A	Kingman
Plusky W	C	Norton
Pounds A	H	Smith Center
Redman A P c	B	St Clair

Name	Co.	Town
Ridlager S	F	Newton
Riddle P G	E	Newton
Reitzel M L s	E	Waterville
Robinson J D	D	Logan
Roy G D	I	Prescott
Scott J W s	K	Leavenworth
Scott J A		South Cedar
Searing C W	H	Pomona
Seward H J c	C	Chatauqua
Shannon C F c	D	Kingman
Shannon C F	D	Newton
Shearer J W	E	Newton
Shamburger S	A	Burlington
Shoemaker J A c	A	Morantown
Sharon J A	E	Wichita
S Ivey J S	E	Valencia
Simmons A A	K	White Rock
Smith D T	A	Plympton
Stott J	M	Abilene
Stevens S	F	Coyville
Taly J H	C	Grand Summit
Terrick G	B	Kennekuk
Tindall A C	E	Baxter Springs
Townsend J M	K	Milan
Turner C R	H	Toledo
Underwood D W	H	Conway Springs
Vennida P	B	Atchison
Wallace M	D	Erie
Ward L B	K	Altamont
Ward A	I	Great Bend
Watt W c	H	Great Bend
Weaver P W	H	Harrison
Webster A B	I	Pleasanton
Wells C A	H	Heber
Williams W M c	H	Great Bend
Wilhite J H	B	Emporia
Willis S c	C	Beattie
Winstead J	E	Chelsea
Yelton J B s	H	Thayer
Zenor B c	I	Stafford

TWENTY-SECOND INFANTRY, THREE YEAR, AND VETERAN.

Col's Jeff. C Davis, M. Gooding, Wm M. Wiles and Thomas Shea.

Name	Co.	Town
Adams R F	K	Neosho Falls
Bell J A c	I	Garnett
Bendure B A	D	Winfield
Beris L W c	F	Great Bend
Blakesley J sgt		Coffeyville
Brazelton J W sgt	A	Salem
Brocker E M	D	Lane
Benham J R	E	Mt. Serratt
Clawson J H	F	Crestline
Cooper W B c	I	Ottawa
Cornwall J G sgt	D	St. John
Coulson T J	C	Arkansas City
Crum T J	H	Michigan Valley
Cunningham W O	I	Arkansas City
Davis G W	K	Superior
Dolsbury C	C	Arkansas City
Earley J A	F	Harveyville
Feh'eison A E	K	Morantown
Fehleison A	K	Wichita
Fidler C	F	Lyona
Fullerton J C	I	Sterling
Goff J B	B	Lincoln
Hall E C	K	North Topeka
Harrison W	D	Glen Elder
Hawks G W	F	Harveyville
Hemphill J B		Clay Center
Herod I E	H	Eureka

Name	Co.	Town
Hildreth G	I	Altamont
Keach J R	B	Valley Center
Kidd J H	B	Richmond
Lewis T M	H	Topeka
Marshall R V lt	C	North Topeka
Matheny J M	C	Topeka
McDaniels J W	E	Carbondale
McDonald R P lt	B	Blue Mound
McIlvane J W	C	Topeka
McIlvane G	C	Augusta
Miller J M	E	Manhattan
Morissey J T c	A	Ft. Scott
Mullen W B		Wichita
Nye Michael	D	Dallas
Pheg'ey H H	F	Eldorado
Rutledge J F	E	Harper
Sage J M	B	Arnold
Sage A T s	B	Arnold
See Wm	A	Florence
Shull A	F	Mulvane
Smith J F	I	Girard
Spears W W	H	Chase
Stewart J	C	Prescott
Tanner M W capt	B	Winfield
Tibbits J N c	I	Barton
Thompson O	E	Burlingame
Traylor J G s m	H	Emporia
Ray H	I	Dodge City

TWENTY-THIRD INFANTRY, THREE YEARS AND VETERAN.

Cols. Wm. L. Sanderson and Geo. S. Babbitt.

Name	Co.	Town
Ansby J	C	Nickerson
Baldwin A	D	Long Island
Bailey L Y	I	Garnett
Benedict H L c	K	Milan
Birch	H	Maud
Bowen R	I	Ellis
Bruner E P 1st lt	K	Emporia
Case G W	C	Milan
Cousins J	I	Chanute
Coyne J F	B	Topeka or Richland
Darst A F c	B	Yates Center
Dougherty F		Scandia
Drake T H	I	Union Center
Fisher A J	D	Weir City
Green C L	F	Round Mound
Guirend W		Mahone
Hallis L	K	Columbus
Harper T	K	Elk
Harris T S	I	White Rock
Hobbs J J 1st lt	A	Beman
Howdyshell I W	H	Dunn
Hungate I	G	Carbondale
Lupton W	D	Howard
Malcolm S	B	Andrew
McNealy J V	D	Topeka
Mitchell B	F	LaCygne
Oehms M	G	Eskridge
Pearson L	C	Chapman
Reynolds R s	I	Paola
Rosier Jacob	I	LaCygne
Rodman W F 1st lt	C	Neosho Falls
Sands R H musician		Baxter Springs
Sawtell Zeph s	E	Montana
Sprague T R	E	Concordia
Staley J	K	Belmont
Staltz J	K	Great Bend
Starwell F H	H	Augusta
Stratton S	E	Walton
Wilhelm J	A	Laura
Woodan S	B	Garnett
Woods R B 1st lt	K	Wyandotte

Wyman D	K	Turon
Wyble S N	G	Chalk Mound
Young P	K	Republic City

TWENTY-FOURTH INFANTRY, 3 YEARS AND VETERAN.

Col's Alvin P. Hovey and Wm. Spicely.

Atkin M M s	I	Fulton
Bitner B	C	Marion
Brooks W C	G	Augusta
Brooks C capt	G	Coffeyville
Campbell G V c	A	Quincy
Carl G		Wamego
Clark Eli	I	Topeka
Dickenson J	C	Humboldt
Erwin Hugh capt	A	Keelville
Fisher T S	K	Virgil
Grase J	A	Walton
Hardman P	I	Belle Plains
Henry J B	K	Nortonville
Hixson J	A	Redfield
Hopkins J A	D	Solomon
Hoggatt J R	B	Quincy
Horton R s	D	Walton
Howard H	E	Smith Center
Huddleson N V	B	Pomona
Hunnell J S	A	Topeka
James N	G	Cheney
Keith Wilson s	D	Topeka
King G E	H	Garnett
Landreth W H	A	Great Bend
Leffler A	B	Great Bend
Legg B M	I	Winfield
Lemmons W W	E	Hunnewell
Mabry C	B	Rock
Miller W M	F	Wilmot
Mitchell W H	K	Sterling
Morricul R L	I	Pottersburg
McAllister G W	K	McCune
Moses J M	F	Lenora
Moyer A	I	Pontiac
Myers J	D	Topeka
Olephant W B s	K	Newton or Parsons
Prather B G	G	Lyndon
Purdy W H	K	Chanute
Raney J M	I	Greely
Ramsey G M	A	Smith Center
Reel T J s	K	LaBette
Rhoads A J	I	Severy
Sanders N	K	Victor
Schmuck P		Hund's Station
Scott J H s	E	Bennington
Sears F A lt col		Pittsburg
Springston A T	H	Empire City
Swingle S P s	K	Florence
Smith J	I	Virgil
Tarr K	I	Girard
Tate G J	B	Scandia
Taylor W P s	G	Yates Center
Trainer K A c	A	Scandia
Wilson W s	D	Polo
Winslow J	G	Garrison
Wolfington J	B	Humboldt
Walker I G	C	Silver Lake

TWENTY-FIFTH INFANTRY, THREE YEARS AND VETERAN.

Cols. James C. Veatch, Wm. H. Morgan and James S. Wright.

Anderson P	H	Topeka
Barnett N W lt	I	Pleasanton
Barrett J N s	F	Wyandotte
Blair R	G	Lyons
Carringer W H	F	Carribon

Name	Co.	Location
Cordry A B	G	Clay C't'r or Baldwin
Cramer John	H	Topeka
Crampton F M lt	H	Galena
Dobbin R	G	Wamego
Cranthain E	B	Dodge City
Graves N	I	Maple Hill
Green W S	B	Ellsworth
Guard N	I	North Topeka
Harrold H	A	Le Roy
Hatfield T	E	Cedarvale
Hathaway D F	I	Venice
Hiatt John	F	Harper
Hutcheson A	K	Melvern
Jones T H s	E	Toronto
Keller J	G	Kindred
Kindred J A	G	Smith Center
Knowlton D	K	McLouth
Logan J E	B	Wellington
Male Aaron	E	Wichita
M ws T	G	Winchester
Mc ney J G	G	Paola
Miller J A	A	Wyandotte
Nilson John capt	G	Smithfield
Nixon M	A	Belle Plaine
Osborn J	C	Rose Hill
Parcells J W	H	Clear Water
Pearson E F	B	Girard
Pinnick E	B	Quincy
Rankin J W	I	Yates Center
Rayfield C	F	Holton
Roseberry J	F	Island
Rucker W G	G	Mound Valley
Skeggs A D	K	Mound Valley
Spellman L	D	Pliny
Weaver P	H	Danville
Whitaker J B	E	Morrow
Whitney D H s	I	North Topeka
White A surgeon		Netawaka
Wright I A	G	Neodesha
Zeigler W M	E	Hays City

TWENTY-SIXTH INFANTRY. THREE YEARS AND VETERAN

Col's Wm. M Wheatley, J. G. Clark:

Name	Co.	Location
Adams	A	Neosho Falls
Barnett W T	A	Iola
Barrett A J s m		Eureka
Barrett H C	C	Nickerson
Ball J H	A	Caldwell
Bicknell A M	B	Altamont
Bicknell	B	Parsons
Boyce C T	F	Clayton
Bowles W W	D	Bunker Hill
Bowers Thos	B	Wilmot
Carter W	A	Rauntoul
Carter H H lt	A	Lyons
Clark A N	B	Betone
Cleland C N	A	Hoyt
Denny S M	C	Leon
Defoe J M	G	Wall Street
Downs E L	H	Grenada
Fernald Chas H	G	Topeka
Forsythe N S	G	Independence
Fowler J W	A	Byron
Fowler H W	I	Lyndon
Galyean M L	A	Salina
Gard W P	H	Mound Valley
Gest L H capt	C	Valley Falls
Griffith J W	C	Bulls City
Hadley L P	E	Hutchinson
Hart G A	D	Paola
Henry J L	D	Summerville
Herron J	G	Thompsonville
Hicks J	F	South Haven

Name	Co.	Town
Hooton J	H	Cow Boy
Hultz J A s	H	Matfield Green
Hupp S S	K	Derry
Huth J N	C	· Manhattan
Johnson J C	C	Soldier
Jones G W	C	Armistead
Jumper A H maj		Melvern
Kelley W A ʾ	E	Galena
Keplinger D	A	Hadley
Leeper C	I	Caldwell
Lenning G G wag'r	F	New Basil
Love W	E	N Lawrence
Love S	E	Harlan
McClanahan A	A	Wamego
McCullough M H s	H	Montana
McDowell J F s	G	Columbus
McDowell C C capt	G	Crestline
McLin J	B	Parsons
McMullen G W lt	K	Melvern
McMullen H B	K	Hutchinson
Mills F M	C	Lane
Mills C	B	Equity
Mills H c	B	Howard
Moberly E S	D	Judson
Morris W W capt	K	Lyndon
Morris I N s	K	La Mont's Hill
Morris A G	K	La Mont's Hill
Munnument G K	K	Afton
Newland J C	G	Cherokee
Paddock M B s	B	Wall Street
Parmer N	D	Bulls City
Pearsall W	I	Louisville
Pellett G W	E	Grass
Poore W	E	Rockville
Purvis F	C	Louisville
Price G	G	Waco
Quick H	B	Topeka
Read E T lt	H .	Oswego
Rice H W lt and q m		Tonganoxie
Rendikrush B M	G	Sedgewick
Roberts D F	D	Pleasanton
Ross Thos	I	Arkansas City
Robb C M c	E	Ivy
Rolfe W	K	Iuka
Roudebush B M	G	Sedgewick
Sherbonda G	A	Brantford
Stambrook D	A	Mound Valley
Stanton W	E	Emporia
Stevenson S E c	B	Parsons
Stott R H capt	H	Columbus
Tillman J W	E	Dover
Tibbett E B	F	Ochiltree
Vanderpool G W	B	Cloverdale
Ward Joel	A	Edna
Wentz M s	E	Piedmont
West S N	G	Elk City
White G	I	Torrance
Wohlford J	A	Centralia
Widener Dan'l	D	Blue Stem

TWENTY-SEVENTH INFANTRY, 3 YEARS
AND VETERAN.
Colonel, Silas Colgrove,

Name	Co.	Town
Achor J P	B	Ottawa
Archer D	D	Hallowell
Arthur C s	F	Sabetha
Arthur B	F	Hepler
Bales W	A	Kirwin
Barnhill R S	G	Louisburg
Berger D	K	Wathena
Bowers T	B	Wilmot
Bradshaw G W 1 s H		Topeka
Bugher A C	B	Spring Creek
Bugher J C	B	Jonesburg

Name	Co.	Location
Bloss J M capt	F	Topeka
Burge G W major	E	Topeka
Burks J H	F	Hartford
Burch W D	F	Cave Springs
Caughron S s	G	Iola
Childs T H	D	Mound Valley
Cooper J A	D	Burlington
Crawford E S	C	Florence
Clark E W	I	Ft Scott
East Geo c	C	Ottawa
Fleanor A	G	Grenola
Fletcher S O	G	Parsons
Greer D G	C	Solomon
Hall W M	I	Thayer
Hannah J C	C	Melrose
Jones J B	E	Columbus
Keck A A	I	Yates Center
Kelso C A I s	G	Grenola
Lawson A J	K	Melvern
List	A	Chanute
Mears W H	E	Peabody
Monett S c	A	Conway
Moore B H	G	Nickerson
Palmer J F	E	Baldwin
Reynolds E E	D	Longton
Richardson E	F	Erie
Scott J	I	Adrian
Sherman J lt	F	Halstead
Shively W L	B	Germania
Squires H	A	Prospect
Swartz E K	I	Hoyt
Tincher G c	A	Topeka
Thornburg E	B	Ashland
Tobias J W	H	Topeka
Watts D B	A	Sedgewick
Weber S F	E	Union City
Wilcoxson J W capt	A	Emporia
Williams J C	F	Junction City
Williams R	D	South Haven

TWENTY–EIGHTH REGIMENT, FIRST CAV-
ALRY, THREE YEARS,

Colonel, Conrad Baker.

Name	Co.	Location
Adams W s	A	Melvern
Adams T M	F	Wellington
Anderson W H s F		Concordia
Andrus W J s	E	Baxter Springs
Aust J	G	Sedan
Baker J	G	Iola
Barrell H	I	N Lawrence
Bates R	F	Caldwell
Billings J	D	Ossawattomie
Bixler M	F	Arvonia
Blades E c	H	Minneapolis
Braden W H s	D	Girard
Bright D	L	Arkansas City
Brown J L	E	Mankato
Calvert J S	F	Leon
Carter J D	G	Norton
Carter J N	E	Earlton
Carter J M	M	Marysville
Chenoweth N c	K	Schoharie
Chirstmass C C	G	Pleasant Dale
Clark W L	B	Princeton
Conley J J	A	Jewell
Courtney J	E	Leanna
Custer John		Harper
Eagles W F	L	Emporia
Elliot H C	H	Wade
Fipps J	I	De Soto
Forbes J c	E	Girard
Foster H	I	Abilene
Garten W D c	C	. Bennington

Name	Co.	Place
Garten J T	C	Solomon
Gittier H	C	Morehead
Goatley 1 P	B	Pawnee Rock
Gowns M	I	Leavenworth
Gordon T	M	Winfield
Green F	I	Longford
Hancock M	L	Scandia
Hare J S	C	Neodesha
Hughes J	G	Lawrence
Jessup S H s	F	Baxter Springs
Jones D M	K	Mound City
Kercheval R P c	B	Girard
Leach J	M	Kingman
Littell W s	D	Center
Marshall W T	I	Wellington
McAllister M V	M	Udall
McElroy K	K	Topeka
McKinney J		Wade
McReynolds W capt	C	Oswego
McWilliams M W	C	Leavenworth
Monroe W	K	N Topeka
Murphy A J	I	Manhattan
Moore T	E	Cheshire
Morris W M	G	Eureka
Outland S	E	Fairmount
Phillips J	G	Harper
Pile H s	K	Wichita
Ray R	K	Harper
Reich C W c	C	Eureka
Schaffer V	A	Lewisburg, Neb
Schooley L	K	Moline
Shaser F	K	Ivy
Smith C C	B	Burlingame
Standley A	L	Madison
Stone D W s	F	Topeka
Talbot W H	C	Eureka
Thomas B F c	B	Emporia
Thomas J	A	Wellington
Torrington J lt	L	Topeka
Tucker W B capt	E	Oswego
Veatch J T lt	F	Columbus
Voorhees Jacob s		Waterville
Walker J L	A	Tipton
Walder S s	B	St John
Watkins W	I	Independence
Winchell S s	D	Silverdale

TWENTY-NINTH INFANTRY, THREE YEARS AND VETERAN.

Col's John F. Miller, David M. Dunn, Samuel O. Gregory.

Name	Co.	Place
Anderson B F	D	Millerton
Aubert A	F	St Marys
Barnes F C	C	Roxbury
Beach F H	A	Beloit
Beach A W	A	Fostoria
Lergner Henry	K	Newton
Bentz J H	B	Peabody
Biddle J	A	Neodesha
Birch G H lt	H	Hutchinson
Bliack C F	C	Enterprise
Black T	E	Topeka
Bockover J L	E	Edmond
Boyd C M	B	Winfield
Boyd J P	B	Maxfield
Brown A c	E	N Topeka
Burdick J	C	Clay Center
Burton W c	I	Auburn
Cline W	K	Dennis
Callahan A W	E	Topeka
Criss M W	B	Topeka
Dennison O J	A	Rosedale
Dilsworth B F ·	I	Columbus

Name	Co.	Residence
Dutcher	F	Farmersburg
Everhart J T	I	Iola
Ferrier J	A	Spearville
Fisher G A	A	Ellsworth
Fouts J A s	E	Osborne
Girard Arthur	D	Blue Springs, Mo
Gillett J W H G	C	Chase
Graves H H	C	Kingman
Greene J D	E	Haddam
Guthrie Hugh	A	Holton
Griffith J C ass't surg		Belleville
Guthrie G E s	A	Eskridge
Hartzog H	K	Winfield
Hazen C J	A	Clyde
Henry J B	K	Nortonville
Hebb E T s	I	Caldwell
Hire Eli	B	Salina
Horton J P hosp steward		Anthony
Hottsdam G L	C	Longton
Johnson J W	C	Columbus
Johnson J E	D	Coffeyville
Knight F	B	St George
Laughton N P	H	Arkansas City
Lees J S	K	Neodesha
Lefy D D	B	Nickerson
Lewis C	G	Arkansas City
Magers G	A	Zara
Maples W	F	Harper or Trenton
McBroom J T	I	Indpendence
McCurdy J q m		Clay Center
McDonald A M	H	Francis
McCowan I lt	A	Orlando
Mitchell B	C	Bloomington
Michael J H s	C	Roxbury
Moore G W lt	B	Winfield
Moore T	G	Haddam
Newhouse L Y	A	Lane
Oliver H	E	Fontana
Parks H S	F	
Pfaff D	I	LaBetre
Phenecie W C	A	Reno
Phenecie Jas	A	Reno
Phenecie Lewis s	A	Reno
Phenecie G W	A	Reno
Quigley Geo W c	F	Moorehead
Rhodes D W	D	Concordia
Roth W	B	Topeka
Richardson A B	C	Iola
Rube J F	B	Labette
Shoupe P s	K	Sedan
Spangle L I s	A	Garnett
Smith D M	G	Sedan
Stinette H	E	Maud
Timmons R M	C	Concordia
Turner Squire	C	Parsons
Van Meter N A	G	Concordia
Wade W	D	Marion
Wallace W	D	Elk City
Webster J E	K	Newton
Wilson J P c	E	Beloit
Wiverly F C	F	Coyville
Wright B F	H	Arlington

THIRTIETH INFANTRY, THREE YEARS AND VETERAN RESIDUARY BATTALION.

Cols. Sion S. Bass, Joseph B. Dodge and Henry W. Lawton.

Name	Co.	Residence
Amos J T	F	Keelville
Anderson R A.	B	Wellington
Asher C B	F	Purity
Baker Wm	G	Burlington
Baker T	E	Avon
Beck A H	K	Winfield

Name	Co.	Town
Benham P	G	Cherryvale
Brady W R	H	Dundee
Broughton C	E	Oak Hill
Brozier J	G	Iola
Brycalton E	B	Fredonia
Buckmaster R	D	Le Roy
Burkdoll J H	A	Welda
Carmine J	B	Arcadia ·
Carter I o-s	A	Leavenworth
Chandler J C	K	Ottawa
DeLano L C	H	Waterville
Daly A S c	C	Cherryvale
Douglas J A	C	Blue Mound
Edsall Peter q m s		Coffeyville
Edsall W	E	Coffeyville
Edsall S A	B	Minneapolis
Ellinwood P o-s	F	Dexter
Fair Charles	E	Alma
Fiddler F	C	Lyona
Fisher J	F	Russell
Ford C R W	C	Centralia
Foss W	E	Newton
Frederickson W	H	Morantown
Godfrey D H	B	Burr Oak
Gugeler W	C	Lyona
Gwynn W H	G	Wellsville
Hass R	C	Neodesha
Homier P s	I	Paola
Hoobes J	A	Harper
Hunt T	K	Equity
Inls Thos	K	Dentonia
Johnson E M	G	Columbus
Johnson G W	B	Washington
Keeler H	H	Cherryvale
Kilgore G W	H	Thayer
Long John	I	Garnett
Longley G W	C	Chetopa
Looby Jacob	K	Cedarvale
Lampman S c	G	Baldwin
Lalley H B s	H	North Topeka ·
Merrifield O s	G	Downs
Messick G c	I	Bodock
Mitchel G B	I	Howard
Moore W H s	G	Miltonvale
Moore L B s maj		Gardiner
Nesbit J M s	D	Princeton
Nolin M K	E	Ossawottamie
Nuef L L	C	Great Bend
Polloek W	C ·	New Basil
Rhodes J H c	E	Colorado
Ritter B F	B	Independence
Scott J	D	Coyville
Shepard J F	G	Effingham
Smalley J D	C	Mound Creek
Smedley J	E	Waterloo
Smith E	E	Oak Hill
Swann R W s	D	Newton
Turner R S	F	Circleville
Whitcomb A	F	Eureka
wilson J H	K	Eldorado
Wilson M S	K	Soldier
Winters H D c	G	Independence

THIRTY-FISRT INFANTRY, THREE YEARS
AND VETERAN.

Col's Chas Cruft, John Osborn, John T.
Smith and James R Hallowell.

Name	Co.	Town
Adams W C	I ·	Iola
Ayers I H capt	D	Wichita
Bales H	D	Chapman
Barley S J c	D	Cherryvale
Blair John lt	I	Parsons
Blair J J		· Parsons

Name	Co.	Residence
Boler J M		Wyandotte
Bonwell W J	F	Winfield
Brockway W	A	Neodesha
Burnett L S	D	South Mound
Clefton S capt	A	Great Bend
Clemons J	K	Minneapolis
Cook A	H	Sternerston
Crabtree W	F	Leon
Cummings O S	I	Leavenworth
Daniel W H	D	Axtell
Dabron W H	H	Radical City
Day John	K	Humboldt
Engle A C	I	Yale
Enlow David c	D	Clay Center
Ferguson R m	H	Parsons
Fryatt A J s	A	Parsons
Garwood G c	E	Axtell
Gilkerson T H	D	Scranton
Gilkinson R B	D	Tower Springs
Godwin J B c	F	Independence
Grey R W	G	Pomona
Hadden D K	G	Elmdale
Hallowell J R col		Wichita
Halstan M s	C	Metz
Hayden C T	H	Cherokee
Helt Joseph	K	Stanton
Hibner John	H	Leonardville
Holliday G W	F	Mulberry Grove
Houston P M	E	Kingman
Hughes John	I	Wayne
Hughes W F	A	Parsons
James W B		Augusta
Johnson D H	J	Fall River
Lamb W H	H	Equity
Laverty J H s	A	Neodesha
Littlejohn A W		Trenton
Maris C F	I	Cloverdale
May M	E	Hutchinson
McKinney A W surg		Hutchinson
Miller J P teamster	D	Cloverdale
Miller John c	A	McCune
Mitchell E T	B	Eldorado
Myers A H	K	Paola
Neal J H	H	McCune
Nelson W H	D	Independence
Parent T H	K	Mound Valley
Pearson J	K	Edna
Peterson J	C	Center
Phillips, P M, c.	D	Sedan
Prinden, W.,	H	Ibaton
Pickens. F. M , capt.,	B	Winfield
Powers, C. A., lt.,	D	Topeka
Scott, J. W .	F	New Salem
Scott, W. H.,	F	New Salem
Setzer, S. H.,	E	Minneapolis
Short, J. A ,	C	Wellington
Slater, Jas., s,	I	Yates Center
Smith, H. A.,	H	Pittsburg
Stewart, F. C.,	F	Independence
Stokes, G C ,	H	N Topeka
Sutherlin, S. H.,	C	Jewell
Sutherlin, M. D.,	C	Scottsville
Swisher, J. G.,	E	Hepler
Waterman, R. H., capt.,	A	Atchison
Welch, W. H. H.,	F	Climax
Wheeler, J. H .	C	Spring Hill
Whitaker, W. W., s.	B	Wilsey
Wilson, F.,	E	Atchison
Wilson, C. C.,	B	Scandia
Winans, Ira, s,	B	Newton
Young, J. C.,	G	Topeka
Young, G. F.,	G	N Topeka
Young, M H.,	C	McPherson

THIRTY-SECOND (FIRST GERMAN) INFANTRY, THREE YEARS AND VETERAN ORGANIZATIONS.

Cols. August Willich, Henry Von Trebra and Francis Erdelmeyer.

Name	Co.	Residence
Bell J W	H	St. John
Benton H E	B	Wamego
Bloom G	C	Clay Center
Bussian C	F	McPherson
Chilling E R	G	Long Island
Cooper T J	D	Newton
Eddy L H capt	C	Everest
Haindel D	F	Delphos
Heigel W	E	Lawrence
Hoelscher H	I	Chase
Igel R S (hosp steward)	B	Leavenworth
Jackson J L	A	Cherokee
Kall L	G	Logan
Klein L	B	Harmony
Maile A	G	Greeley
Shields J D	A	Norwood
Shilling E drummer	G	Logan
Stiltzner E	C	Pleasant Run
Taff David c	D	Custer
Trebra Von L capt	E	Chetopa
Wall W J	C	Xenia
Wick Michael	F	Normanville
Wright G W	A	Sycamore Springs
Wright James	A	Sycamore Springs

THIRTY-THIRD INFANTRY, THREE YEARS AND VETERAN.

Cols. John Coburn and James E. Burton.

Name	Co.	Residence
Albright John c	A	Princeton
Alexander A H	H	Topeka
Banister S	B	(dec'd) Topeka
Bart S A	I	Coffeyville
Bartley A H	B	Lamar
Bass K S	H	Bennington
Benford C F	B	Wichita
Best Geo	A	Coyville
Bledso P W	B	Pomona
Britton Geo		Republic City Neb
Brannan T J	D	Grantville
Bromwell J F c	C	Antelope
Brown J M s	D	North Topeka
Brown D F	A	Central City
Burch J W	B	Ft. Scott
Bust J H	I	Coffeyville
Brown Seth	E	Harveyville
Coleman W	I	Parsons
Council O	D	Augusta
Crane J A	K	Equity
Crage R B s	G	Medicine Lodge
Curns N	E	Pleasanton
Carney W H	G	Strawn
Chandler W capt	D	Topeka
Dolsby Martin	G	Haddam or Cuba
Duffey E drummer	D	Leon or Sterling
Duncan H W	F	Baxter Springs
Drum W H	C	Wichita
Esten W D	H	Concordia
Esten W M	E	Hepler
Evans Thos	D	Minneapolis
Farmer W D	K	Topeka
Fields R	A	Iola
Francis J	I	Halstead
Furnish B F	B	Valley Center
Garber W	G	Scandia
Gleason D	I	Kinsley
Glessner T F s	C	Pioneer
Goodrick A T	K	Fowler

Gurley J T	C	Wellington
Gwynn J F	E	North Topeka
Halbert E capt	I	Beloit
Hawkins, T c,	I	Grenola
Haynes, W. L.,	K	Topeka
Hendricks, L· T.,	K	Cloverdale
Harrington, T., s,	F	Atchison
Hinton, G.,	F	Jackson
Hinkle, J. B.,	A	Emporia
Hoding, A., c,	D	Wichita
Hopkins, W. H.,	K	Chase
Hubbard, J. M.,	G	Dodge City
Hubbard, Isaac,	G	Dodge City
Hunter, Geo.,	F	Jackson
Hunter, J. C.,	A	Burr Oak
Jamison, J.,	C	Havana
Johnson, Phillip		Ft Scott
Johnson, Shelby, s,	D	Baxter Springs
Johnson P	C	Independence
Jones John c	A	Coyville
Keeler A R	I	Clay Center
Keene S	F	Wilsey
Kern J S	K	Litchfield
King Joseph.	G	Woodville
Kirkham H H	A	Ridgeway
Laws Isaac	A	Chelsea
Lee J C	H	Wellington
Lippert G W	C	LaCrosse
Loller I J	H	Liberty
Lyons H H lt	E	Ft Scott
Lyness E M	H	Walnut
Mansfield J W	G	Arkansas City
Mather W	K	Topeka
Maze J C major		Topeka
McCloud W	A	Elk City
McCloud J A	A	Ballard's Falls
McConnell W	G	Armourdale
McDonald P H	F	Ashland
Mitchell J E	C	Montana
Mofieth J	K	Wyandotte
Moore, B	D	Frankfort
Monroe P A s	B	Tonganoxie
Meyers Geo	G	Millwood
Myers Jacob	H	Moline
Newby, A S	B	Topeka
Orner Geo D s	C	Garden City
Orner W H H	C	Hiawatha
Overton L	H	Pomona
Pauland A		Udall
Pearce R C	A	Melrose
Polk I C	F	Mound City
Polk F M	F	Mound City
Pray E T	A	Osawatomie
Prescott B H	C	St John
Pruden L	C	LeCompton
Regnier P J	I	Kinsley
Reed Joel	K	Sternerton
Rattabaugh J R	E	Dodge City
Russell O J s	H	Emporia
Shoemaker J T	A	Muscotah
Shelton G W	A	Godfrey
Six J L	K	Ft Scott
Smith, J W	I	Harveyville
Squires H	A	Scandia
Stipe M W	B	Redden
Strack P J	I	Junction City
Stufflebeam M	K	Kansada
Sturgeon T R	E	Rush Center
Swisher J S	C	Xenia
Taylor J R	H	Topeka
Taylor Thos	H	Baldwin
Thomason W C	K	Concordia
Thorne Geo	B	Mt Hope

Van Horne B	K	Wyandotte
Wagner W	B	La Bette
Wall W J	C	Morantown
Ward E	C	Seneca
Watson G W	K	Topeka
Welch S H	K	Allegan
Widner E F s	E	Anthony
Williams H E	I	Morantown
Worth F W	C	Silver Lake

THIRTY-FOURTH INFANTRY, THREE YEARS AND VETERAN

Cols. Asbury Steele, Townsend Ryan, Robt.
A. Cameron, Robt. B. Jones and
Robt. G. Morrison.

Abney Wm		Morehead
Atkin J H	D	Mankato
Bartlow O W	A	Lyle
Becker J T	C	Glen Elder
Bell T N	D	Burlington
Bohrer Godfrey	D	Chase
Boone C D	F	Lincoln
Coan S P	H	Medicine Lodge
Cole H	F	New Haven
Cusler James c	B	Perth
Dawson G c	K	Winfield
Denny G W	b	Halstead
Divelbiss Jonas	C	Melvern
Evans J E	I	Galena
Evers Elias c	I	Hutchinson
Fortner H lt	K	Wichita
Fulton A C lt	A	Olathe
Furnish J F	F	Wichita
Garrett J M c	H	Manhattan
Griffith M L	D	Chanute
Grinwell J L asst surg		Peabody
Hale Harvey	K	Caldwell
Hodson J	C	Burr Oak
Houseman G W	G	Paxico
Houser J W	H	Paradise
Houser A A c	H	Paradise
Irwin S R lt	C	North Topeka
James Evan	G	Cambridge
Johnson John		Wichita
Jones D H	I	Tower Springs
Kearns T c	C	Phillipsburg
Kelsey T C	C	Abilene
Kritcher J W	D	Lecompton
Kever Martin	F	Stewart
Kirtley B F	C	Lyner
Knapp G W	K	Cedarville
Kreigh E		Grover
Kuhns G W	A	Ft Scott
Lucas N W c	H	Fredonia
Manning E C	D	Newton
May Lewis	K	Mankato
May J R	B	Marion
McConthey F C	C	Howard
McCrackin W D	C	Howard
Mitchell W	C	Mound City
Moore Thos	E	Great Bend
Mott Geo	I	Clay Center
Neil W	I	Parsons
Noble J A	D	Derby
Nolder A B c	B	Maxville
Pickard J G	D	Arkansas City
Pickard Joseph	D	Arkansas City
Piersol E M	E	Williamsburg
Pollenbarger R	K	Larkin
Plasterer W A m	G	Smith Center
Pugh Albert	B	Smith Center
Richards Geo W	C	Belle Mead

Shull John	B	Clifton
Smith H C H o	K	Carlton
Sims H W	A	Coffeyville
Spaulding O A	I	Tower Springs
Spring B A	K	Burlington
Stine H W	A	Coffeyville
Stroll Geo	A	Ellsworth
Studley C W	E	Chetopa
Swallow I A	B	Stuart
Swallow W W	B	Stuart
Swan L C c	F	Independence
Tanquary R K	K	Neodesha
Templar A M capt	B	Williamsburg
Thomas Wm c	H	Parsons
Thomas J H	H	Peabody
Thomas S L	D	Myers Valley
Thompson J F	F	Seneca
Twibell Thos	I	Pottersburg
Waymire J	E	Wall Street
Webster E D c	K	Holton
Welty Aaron s	H	Wamego
Williams W E	K	Medicine Lodge
Woodard W B	D	Coyville
Woodyard John	K	Holton
Woodyard W	K	Havensville

THIRTY-FIFTH INFANTRY (OR FIRST IRISH,)
3 YEARS.

Colonels—John C. Walker, Bernard F. Mullen, August G. Tassin

Alvey J H s	D	Twin Creek
Barrett James s	G	Osborne
Baugher John	I	Jetmore
Blue David I	D	Bell
Butler S S 1st s	I	Columbus
Cahill Thomas lt	K	Fall River
Cart W H	D	Almena
Chamberlain D R	I	Burlingame
Chance J W	K	Ashland
Curl S A	B	Oswego
Ditman J F c	F	Sedan
Flynn Wm lt	K	Topeka
Glazier L	G	Box City
Haney J M	D	Dodge City
Hamer Henry		Green
Hosehatt John capt	D	Ft Leavenworth
Hyde L E capt	K	New Albany
Hyde L B c	K	Turett
Jordon James	D	Lyndon
Justice S M	C	Hollensburg
King Wm	F	Garnett
Kendall W H	B	Youngstown
Luka Fred	K	Abilene
McAllister Joel	F	Elmira
Mock W H	D	Bristow
Murray A J	I	Seneca
Parsons G W asst surg		Robinson
Rea W B	H	Dillon
Robbins Eppah	G	Halstead
Robbins Geo	G	Russell
Self J	F	Altamont
Sheffield C H	I	Delphos
Sutton Amos	F	Twin Falls
Sweet S L	D	Cedarvale
Valandigham J A c	H	Toronto
Whallen J J	I	Hazleton
Westrap J T	E	Hope
Wood Robt	A	Netherland
Younker James	F	Eskridge

THIRTY-SIXTH INFANTRY, THREE YEARS AND VETERAN.

Cols William Grose and O. H. P. Carey.

Adamson E H	D	Lenora
Allen Wm	A	Manhattan
Anderson J H	F	Okaw
Palmer J L	I	Hays City
Cautley G M lt	D	Wichita
Curry F G	E	Eudora
Dawson Isaac	A	Clyde
Deselms W B	C	Mound City
Diggs F C	F	Noble
Essex John	B	Burlington
Freeman L C capt	A	Cecil
Grove A H	E	Newton
Hamline O T	G	Lamont's Hill
Haney M	C	Sedgwick
Hays Noah	E	Seneca
Heacock E E	A	Anthony
Hewitt Joseph	K	Cherryvale
Hiatt Joel	C	Chester Neb
Hoover J M	E	Galesburg
Hunt H P	E	Coffeyville
Jenkins Joseph	E	Byron
Johnson James	F	Yates Center
Jones John	H	State Center
Judy D H	E	Concordia
King S G		Cedarville
Leeka M	B	Jack
Lemon E J c	F	Ft. Scott
Limpus W T cap		Olathe
Manis C	A	Coffeyville
Miller Matthew	I	Havensville
Modlin W S c	C	Rose
Mullen Hugh L		Fowler
Mallory H C	G	Leavenworth
Newby D c	A	Howard
Pike S F	D	More Sod Barton Co
Pitts J S		Dowell
Reed David	F	Girard
Snowden S	G	Conway
Spangler John	B	Menoken
Sparks F M c		Springdale
Stevens C C	F	Walnut
Thornburg J s	B	Equity
Walker W F		Wichita
Weber W H	C.	Akron
Young David		Mound Valley

THIRTY-SEVENTH INFANTRY, THREE YEARS AND VETERAN.

Cols. Geo. W. Hazzard, Carter Gazlay and James S. Hull.

Ard Jacob	F	Osage City
Birdwell M m band		Green
Beck F c	E	Big Timber
Brown F F	B	Mound Valley
Brown J E	B	Liberty
Busby J P	F	Wichita
Caroine J M c	F	Spearville
Cole Wm c	A	Dora
Cowan S H	H	Louisburg
Cox T J c	I	Rossville
Dalrymple C L	A	Council Grove
Elrod W D s	A	Reading
Grecian Isaac	A	Bulls City
Hampton H L	A	Glenn
Hanna David	D	Howard
Henry J S lt		Russell
Hinds F M		Atchison
Hodges C E		Meriden

Name	Co.	Place
Hopkins W E		Topeka
Hughes Addis	E	Topeka
Hungate A J lt	E	Topeka
Johnson W F	C	Rossville
Kelley R J	C	Harper
Kennett Jas	C	Pleasant Run
Lawson J B	A	Kingman
Loser Wm	E	Columbus
McCracken T F s	H	Kingman
Morton John	C	Pawnee City Neb
Myers Wm	C	North Topeka
Osborne J C	A	Beloit
Owens John	I	Ellworth
Pye Geo W capt	H	Cherokee
Reser J H c	C	Rossville
Reser M	C	Rossville
Roberts J K c	1	Pleasanton
Snook M J	H	Delphos
Souter S O	G	Parsons
Stark J B	D	Center Ridge
Thompson J M	B	Cactus
Van Meter T G	B	Glen Elder
White T J s	I	Elk City
Wilkenson I	B	Parkerville
Wise James c	D	Lawrence
Wooley J H s	E	Constant

THIRTY EIGHTH INFANTRY, THREE YEARS AND VETERAN.

Cols. Benjamin F. Scribner, Daniel F. Griffin and David H. Lown.

Name	Co.	Place
Adams A W	B	Morehead
Apple M N	A	Burden
Alenger H	D	Chase
Banks Elisha	A	Roxbury
Benton H E	A	Wamego
Bonwell A	B	Metz
Boyer James	D	Hess
Boyer J H c	D	Hess
Cady A O	F	Wellsville
Crandall Floyd c		Reserve
Delano Geo C	H	Scottsville
Forbes James	D	Girard
Fuller Watson	I	Buffalo
Gailer Robt P	D	Colony
Gray P J	H	Edna
Haney Milton	D	Sedgwick
Hiller C S s	F	Wyandotte
Hubbard J G s	C	Galena
Keeper P M s m	C	Beaumont
Kenyon W A	A	Ackerlund
Lacy J A	E	Burton
Lemert J	I	Newton
Lenean W L capt	B	Sedan
Lenean J I s	B	Gaylord
Leonard W capt	I	Baldwin
Light Isaac T s	C	Sarensburg
Lindsay J P	A	Pomona
Lopp C W capt	B	Columbus
Lukenbill T B	G	Cherryvale
Marshall Eli	D	Garnett
Mauck F S s	B	Strawn
McAllister Geo	K	McCune
McCormick W C	G	Wilmot
McCormick S H	G	Salt City
Michaels A	E	Grand Center
Milligan J W	H	Topeka
Mosier Joseph	G	Lenora
Nesbit J H	D	Pottawatomie
Nunemacher C B capt	B	Ashland

Primmer D A   capt   E   Burden
Pinnick W D   o   I   Baxter Springs
Reed T J   C   Altamont
•Russell Thos   C   Muscotah
Seacat W L wagoner   K   Winfield
Stuart A   A   Garnett
Stewart J E   I   Newton
Spencer P   B   Thayer
Summons G W   K   Hosford
Thompson M H   D   Stuart
Vaczante W   A   Parsons
Ward G W R   I   Menoken
Webb G W   capt   A   Galena
Wilson Riley   K   Wellington
Young C C   H   Sedan

THIRTY-NINTH REGIMENT—EIGHTH CAVALRY 3 YEARS AND VETERANS.

Colonels—Thomas J. Harrison and Fielder A. Jones.

Applegate J A q m s   B   Lyons
Baldwin W L   C   Grenola
Benton J H   K   Vining
Bickle Wm   G   Matthewson
Bodle P S   C   Clearwater
Boyer J E capt   E   LaCrosse
Brannan D J   A   Peabody
Barns James Hosp Steward J   Iola
Burris J F 1st s   A   Topeka
Bush D W   A   Walnut
Cain Thos   M   Burlingame
Campbell Thos   E   Argentine
Cody A O   F   Wellsville
Crump H C s   F   Manhattan
Cody B G capt   F   Wellsville
Dalby L   L   Oswego
Dalrymple T   C   Minneapolis
Durkate J S   H   Independence
Ellis B F   K   Truman
Ellis J K   D   Lerado
Fisher C H   E   Concordia
Foust C J   L   Fall Leaf
Furgison W P   B   Waseca
Gates John   I   Ashville
Gillespie R J   K   Skiddy
Hall Wm capt   E   New Albany
Hardy John   M   Mendota
Harrison J N   K   Ottawa
Higbee H B   B   Beaumont
Hinkle D M   A   Oskaloosa
Haden J   F   Seneca
Hancock F M   K   Edna
Jackson A 1st lt   C   Cawker City
Johnson Jabin   B   Cottonwood Falls
Johnson J C   L   Oswego
Johnson Jasper   M   Garfield
Johnson John   B   Valley Center
Keffer Eli c   E   Wichita
Keller M s   M   Delphos
Kelley H W   F   Newton
Knee B. F   G   Eldorado
Kreller J M   H   Ivy
Leppert W   K   Dodge City
Lett J T   D   Garfield
Lindsay J C   D   Hutchinson
Lock W M s   F   Newton
Love H B   A   Robinson
Madison I   F   Rosalia
Masters J L   I   Parsons
Martin W   B   Great Bend

Name	Co.	Place
Matlock John c	M	Independence
Mallenbruch H I c	F	Morrill
Mooney Robert s	G	New Albany
Moore P c	F	Wetmore
Moore W H	C	Winfield
McClary S	K	Ibaton
McKee B F	A	Torrance
Newby P E	M	Oxford
Nickolson J lt	F	Grenola
Nuckels A R	C	Oak Hill
Phillips C W s	I	Tonganoxie
Platner C	M	Kingman
Pound D R		Stafford
Purvis A L	G	Block
Railsback J T s	L	Atchison
Richmond W	C	Rest
Ring Garret	F	Eldorado
Rolf W J.	C	Pittsburg
Ross W B	G	Plympton
Russell J K	K	Mound
Schock H J	E	Chetopa
Shewalter S H 1st s	G	Eureka
Shirley Thos	E	Ingalls
Strive Martin	I	Dennis
Slusher Wm s	L	Garnett
Smith J S	H	Dodge City or Harper
Smith J R	M	Simpson
Somers S	D	Centerville
Spaulding H H lt	F	Glasco
Stanley Frank c	C	Alliance
Stevens W	L	Chetopa
Stewart W H	A	Severance
Study Wm s	E	Cedarvale
Thomas A B	L	Olathe
Thomas J W	B	Fall Leaf
Thompson G G	H	Abilene
Tolie J R	H	Severy
Tomlinson J Q	F	Winfield
Ulmer Geo W	K	Osborne
Watkins J P	M	Welda
Watkins L F	M	Hiawatha
Watts J S	A	Rock
Wall W K	E	Belmont
Wall S G c	E	Belmont
Wallace E O s	E	Oneida
Walters J W	G	Elk City
Ward W D s	D	Garfield
Windle R E	E	Arkansas City
Winchell Z c	L	Bashan
Winters Geo T capt	U	Chapman
Wilkinson I	B	Parkersville
Welchel J	E	Concordia
Whitson A	K	Garden City
Worden J B s	C	Warrensburg, Mo

FORTIETH REGIMENT INFANTRY 3 YEARS: AND VETERANS.

Colonels, Wm. C. Wilson, John W. Blake and Henry Leaming.

Name	Co.	Place
Adams J M	B	Osawkee
Allen Joseph	G	Kingman
Arbuckle W H	E	Red Cloud Neb
Barnes Erastus		N Topeka
Beatty P T	C	Hutchinson
Bell Ambrose	C	Eureka
Bloth D G		Rosedale
Brown L J	D	Junction City
Buck N Y lt	B	Olivet
Burris W s	F	Peru
Carter A C	I	Barnesville

Cline S T	F	Eureka
Conk W A	H	Lowe
Conwell S A	I	N Topeka
Cottrell Albert	I	Morrill
Curnett W W s	G	Neodesha
Edwards Wm s	F	Conway
Ellis R W	C	Dallas
Embree A S	A	Manhattan
Fletcher D M	F	Fredonia
Foster S C	I	Osage City
Garver W L	I	Harlan
Gault W D	C	Humboldt
Gault A L	C	Humboldt
Goldsberry T M capt	D	Conway
Gourley J H	B	Cawker City
Hahn Joseph	B	Oxford
Hamilton W A s	G	Oskaloosa
Heaton Robt o	B	Cresson
Heaton J E	D	Olathe
Hedrick M V B m		Russel
Heron Arthur	D	Mound Valley
Hibbs John	I	Elsinore
Horton Wm	E	Arnold
Kirkpatrick C H capt	G	Albuquerke N M
Kelso J A	C	Liberty
Kelly W H	G	Chanute
Kennedy A		Independence
Kitchen James capt	C	Englewood
Knetzer C B	D	Erie
Kohler Peter	E	Sedgewick City
Lewis J N	F	Burlington
Mather G W	G	Antrim
McCoy J D	K	Pawnee Rock
McIntosh G W	H	Council Grove
McMasters H s	I	Cloverdale
Miller John c	A	Wellington
Mills H C c	C	Osborne
Moratt J A	B	Meriden
Myers W C	A	Milton
Neff Elias col		Winfield
Owens D R P	B	Altoona
Peddicord N F	H	Baldwin
Redden I P	I	Soldier
Richardson D H s	I	Belmont
Ross J W	G	Wichita
Slavens H	G	Greeley
Smith G B	F	Normanville
Spencer J B	E	Pottersburg
Thompson W A	H	Cactus
Thompson J R	C	Cactus
Thornell L s	C	Girard
Tull W F	A	Leon
Weaver S capt	H	Morrill
Wills H c	B	Kingman
Winner W C lt	D	Fredonia
Woolman B	K	Seneca
Woolpert M	B	North Topeka
Winmore G W	C	Humboldt
York P	G	Topeka
Young John	F	Ozark
Yount W F	I	Pomona

FORTY FIRST REGIMENT, SECOND CAVALRY,
3 YEARS, VETERANS.

Colonels— J. A. Bridgland, R. N. Hudson
E. M. McCook, James W. Stewart.

Alexander J	L	Sunnydale
Arnold A J	G	North Topeka
Arnott Thos	G	Topeka
Barber H S	K	Independence

Name		Place
Beard Jesse s	H	Elk Falls
Beaumont D C	D	Argentine
Booth Chas	A	Bronson
Borders John	H	Elk City
Brinker W R capt	E	Alida
Buchanan John	E	Fontana
Buckley Wm	A	Chetopa
Byroad D M	H	Sharon
Carter Geo	I	Osage City
Combs Job	D	Newton
Conway H J w m	A	Arkansas City
Cook Virgil A s maj		North Topeka
Cooper Horace	M	Beloit
Crain Eugene lt	H	Belle Mead
Cray R A	D	Peabody
Crow James	I	Prosper
Darnall L J lt	B	Silver Dale
Easter D M	B	Scranton
Eidson A M	K	Reading
Evans A H lt	K	Ellsworth
Faust Aaron	G	McCune
Fetters W P	A	Kalamazoo
Gilbert W H c	F	Oxford
Goldsborough H J c	H	Lorette
Graves John	B	Douglas
Gray Hiram	C	Fawn Creek
Gurtler F N	B	North Topeka
Haskin M S	A	La Dore
Hathaway C E	M	Wamego
Hoover D N	C	Burlington
Howell H	B	Farlington
Hudson B	D	Ft Scott
Huffington Geo	H	McCune
Johnson J T	G	Kansas City, Ks
Jones W B	E	Parsons or LaBette
Judd Wm	A	Oswego
Keenan J W	D	Lyndon
Kums F B e		Caldwell
Kyle Hiram	E	Turner
Lamb John	H	Wellington
Lassell E W c	C	Sunnydale
Leabo J S capt	G	Guilford
Leabo John lt	K	Sedan
Loveland L J*	A	Clay Center
Madlaner J	F	Wellington
Manker L	D	Topeka
Madden Thos c	B	Florence
McClure J M s	I	Milan
McCabe W M s	M	Portis
McCall	B	North Topeka
McCullough J C	B	Altamont
McGonigal W C lt	K	Beloit
Moser John c	K	Bulls City
Parker H W	A	Scranton
Phaebus M	M	Cadmus
Plantze L	K	Holton
Robinson Wm	B	Delta
Robinson Wm	G	Caney
Russell J F	A	North Topeka
Smith J hosp steward		Parsons
Smith H	H	Kingsley
Sproat G A	C	Hutchinson
Stone W D s	F	Topeka
Sweet J M	B	Rosedale
Thomas W E	E	Carlyle
Thompson G R	A	Moran own
Trickler A farrier	L	Rest
Webb F M	A	Dennis
Weaver Levi c	M	Ashton
Wells G W s	D	Scandia

Name	Company	Place
White F B	F	Ottawa
Williams J B capt	R	Osage City
Yaple Oscar	H	Hardy Neb
Wright W B	D	Topeka

FORTY-SECOND INFANTRY, THREE YEARS AND VETERAN.

Cols. James G. Jones, W. T. B. McIn'yre, Gid R. Kellams.

Name	Company	Place
Barnevel G B	E	Tyner
Benefield Isaac	D	Longton
Bowser Chas R	E	North Cedar
Brown Dan L	B	Concordia
Calkins W T	B	Parsons
Carpenter J	C	Holton
Casteel Eli	A	Keightly
Childers J A	D	Larned
Cookson E	I	Winfield
Dunmick G F	C	Hanover
Ellis J W	G	Silver Lake
Enlow Elijah lt	B	Pavilion
Freeman S	H	Severance
Gerard Wm	F	Emporia
Glaze W S	E	Anthony
Glickman Geo	A	Hutchinson
Gregory W F s	G	Winfield
Gregory Jere	G	Baltimore
Haas A	H	Glen Sharrald
Harding W D	A	Twin Mound
Helder P C s major		Manhattan
Herman C	B	Lyons
Jackson T J lt	B	Newton
Hendrickson A F	R	Jamestown
Hill C W	H	Louisville
Johnson Lewis	E	Arkansas City
Johnson W B	E	Arkansas City
Johnson James	G	Baltimore
Kettle J W	C	Haverhill
Martin J M c	K	Parsons
McCoy E	B	Pittsburg
Miller Wash	A	Oswego
Park Geo W	F	Sunnydale
Parrott M c	A	Wichita
Penner Hugh lt	I	De Soto
Pitts Frank	B	Garfield
Post J M	A	Woodbury
Preston John	K	Oberlin
Shook Geo T lt	C	Wyandotte
Shuyler J A	C	Sterling
Stark G P	B	Bitlertown
Stonacher B S	B	Lyndon
Tegmeier	C	Manhattan
Walker W H	A	Columbus
Wilkinson Levi c	B	Topeka

FORTY-THIRD REGIMENT INFANTRY, THREE YEARS AND VETERAN.

Cols. Geo. K. Steele, W. E. McLean, John C. Major.

Name	Company	Place
Albaugh Edward	F	Phillipsburg
Alexander J D	H	Topeka
Allen James P	B	Erie
Andrews J W lt	I	Pine Grove
Bacon James F	I	Mentor
Ball W H c	K	Garden Plains
Band A B	I	Spearville
Baysinger W A	G	Hartford
Beatty John	C	Jonesburg
Bell James A	G	Lyle
Birch A I	E	Center
Boyle C F asst surg		Earlton

Name	Co.	Place
Brown J A	A	South Haven
Browning W A	B	Chanute
Burcham Reuben	C	Fulton
Burnside D W	B	Chetopa
Calhoun C	I	Irving
Calvert J D	C	Irving
Carey W C	D	Lawrence
Cooprider Presly	A	Willard
Cowgill J W	H	Princeton
Crist Isaac	I	Matfield Green
Cromwell S T s	A	North Topeka
Cropper John	H	Armourdale
Conaway B N	G	Salem
Cullison R c	C	Cana
Cullison I	C	Garnett
Dixon Zimri	K	Crestline
Duval J M	E	Climax
Denyer M	G	Independence
Ellis J B	K	Minerva
Ewing Robert	H	Clarksburg
Frazier C N	K	Lawrence
Fugate J W	A	Richmond
Garrigus S P s	K	Carbondale
Gibson A W c	B	Blue Rapids
Goolman J W	H	North Topeka
Gordon Isaac	C	Vermillion
Graham D E	K	Le Roy
Gray Wm	K	Parsons
Hadley J W s	K	Smith Center
Hargrave G W	B	Independence
Harrel W N s	H	Blue Mound
Harris B R	D	Corning
Husbam Mc H	A	Scranton
Ingle E S	B	Sedan
Jackson Henry	C	Box City
Jackson J W	F	Osage City
Johns J B	C	Salina
Johns J M capt	G	Salina
Johnson C M s	G	Alma
Jones J B	C	Oswego
Knapp Peter	B	Wathena
Lara A J	K	Burlington
Lasley W	B	Xenia
Layton J	D	Galena
Logan D M	D	Ft. Scott
Logan E S s	D	Morehead
Long G W	I	Edgecomb
Lovelace J P s	D	Coffeyville
Martin W L lt	G	Winfield
McCarr James	F	Erie
McCutcheon M M c K		Parsons
McKee	E	Cana
Mitchell E	K	Cottonwood Falls
Moore F J lt	K	Akron
Moore Harrison c	E	Colorado
Muir T G	B	Carbondale
Murphy W	A	Havensville
Myers Chas	D	Walton
Ockerman John	C	Geneva
O'Conner John	K	Girard
Osborn J F	E	Junction City
Osborn Silas	E	Junction City
Painter W W	K	Winfield
Peters W D	C	Lyons
Pierson J E	H	Watson
Riddle W H	H	Pomona
Roach S T capt	E	Garnett
Robertson Wm		Omio
Seeds Jesse	I	Wellington
Smith Job	E	Burlington
Sparks B F	F	Colorado
Sparks J D	F	Colorado
Spencer J F	B	Burlington

Spencer J K	B	Greeley
Stalker G W	F	Hartford
Stoker Wm	I	Independence
Sutherland J A	C	Caldwell
Thomas Lyman s	B	Greeley
Tippin J S	B	Greeley
Tippin Thos	B	Greeley
Tittsworth C G	K	Coffeyville
Uhl Geo	G	Cedar Junction
Usrey Philip	E	Baxter Springs
Walker W H	A	Oswego
Williamson T W lt	B	LaCygne
Wilson J H	B	Neosho Falls
Winkler M V B	K	Fawn Creek
Woody Wm	C	North Topeka

FORTY-FOURTH REGIMENT INFANTRY, THREE YEARS, VETERAN.

Cols. Hugh B. Reed, Wm. C. Williams, Simeon C. Aldrich, James F. Curtis.

Aldrich J L	A	Rooks Center
Aldrich F H	A	Rooks Center
Aultman H H c	K	Parsons
Aumsbaugh H s	G	Rice
Barsch Adam	E	Brooks
Blough Philip	H	Halstead
Brown B	D	Melville
Burnworth C	E	Rockwell City
Carl B S Mc	C	Reece
Clevenger B F	B	Caldwell
Coder John	I	Minneapolis
Colgrove H P		Chase
Dodge John	C	Jordan Springs
Dotts Jesse	A	Garnett
Dotts Jacob	A	White Cloud
Farmer Wm	D	Concordia
Fisher V B	H	Seneca
Freeby G W	F	Barnes
Gibson John	F	Kansas Center
Gibson I C	D	Millerton
Gleggy B	H	Halstead
Groves Geo	F	Independence
Guthrie Levi	K	Cope
Hanslip E W	H	Osage City
Hartsel Samuel	D	Oxford
Hinds J J	C	Le Roy
Hoagland James	H	Ellsworth
Humphrey Z	I	Clayton
Johnson W E	I	Baltimore
Johnson J W	D	Iola
Jones Smith	E	Star Valley
Krieble Noah	I	Olivet
Jackson W F	E	Neosho Falls
Lomax Junius	H	Mound City
Maple R	F	Green
McCurdy S c	F	Whiting
McIntyre Benj c	B	Otega
McLinnis Marion	C	Alcona
Moore T J	K	La Bette
Myers C P	E	Parsons
Muphy J P	G	Safford
Pimlat C D	E	Augusta
Read J V	D	Carbondale
Rhoads Henry s	E	Gardner
Robbins J c	E	Pratt
Robbins J Y	E	Alta
Schamp R G	F	New Haven
Schoonover E H s B		Newton
Scovill Hannibal	A	Columbus
Sherburn W lt	B	Oxford
Smith Harvey s	B	Burden
Spears W T	H	Junction City
Spencer A J	D	Saratoga

Snyder Wm K	H	Richland
Strape A J	F	Nickerson
Stroup Fred s	I	Media
Sutton J c	H	Towanda
Totten T B c	F	Huntsville
Van Ness A	B	Galva
Waybill S T	D	Mound Valley
Yates John	D	Leonardsville

FORTY-FIFTH REGIMENT, THIRD CAVALRY, THREE YEARS VETERANS.

Colonels—Scott Carter, Geo. H. Chapman.

Adams F M lt	I	Linnwood
Applegate Ira lt	G	Lyons
Barton W H	F	Harper
Begny R S lt	D	Lancaster
Brown Chas lt	I	Pottawattomie
Brown H V s	G	Hunnewell
Brown James	E	Chetopa
Bryant Samuel	L	Lawrence
Burton M M	I	Haddam
Carr V S	D	Longton
Clark Jesse C	M	Olean
Cline John H	D	Chapman
Cole D R s	D	White Church
Cook James W	H	Burlington
Cook Conrad	A	St George
Cooper A	C	Topeka
Cooper Silas		North Topeka
Cooper W M	I	Melvern
County P H	G	Cactus
Cracraft W F	I	Arkansas City
Cranston Thomas s	A	McCune
Danglade J B	C	Baxter Springs
Furney L A	G	Baldwin
Folmer J M	G	Parsons
Funk David	B	Abilene
Gasaway J S s	E	Spring Hill
Green L H	B	Benton
Harris L W s	C	Baxter Springs
Havs A O	A	Matfield Green
Herriott J J F s	G	Dover
Hopp Aaron	H	Arkansas City
Hughs H	E	Neosho Rapids
Johnson G W	H	Sharps Creek
Johnson C M s	G	Alma
Lancaster W M	A	Lousburg
Lewis A F	F	Elk City
Lowry J	B	White Rock
Matthews W N	H	Benton
Maudlin J	E	Scandia
McClung D F		Harper
McKee J T	E	Morehead
McKinney W A	D	Ophir
McNeal Wm	E	Lancaster
Monfort P S	I	Neodesha
Moore P S s	K	Independence
Morris W H	D	Canton
Murphy J H	M	Arcadia
Plummer J W	H	Keene
Rathert H	M	Alida
Reeve H C	F	North Topeka
Shultz John	I	Hutchinson
South David s	F	North Topeka
Spangler John	B	Menoken
Sterling Chas	K	Longton
Sterritt J H s	F	Monroe
Tilton A J s	L	Kansas City
Trotter M L	B	Parsons
Urmy S S	F	North Topeka
VanOsedel I N	A	Cedar Point

Vannice J B	A	North Topeka
Vanness A	B	Galva
Wallace G O s	I	Leona
Webster D G	F	Eureka
Wetherald John	H	Springdale
Winchell Z	L	Arkansas City
Younker B H s	D	Mission Creek

FORTY–SIXTH REGIMENT INFANTRY THREE YEARS VETERANS.

Colonels; G N Fitch and Thomas H. Bringhurst.

Adair Austin	B	Bonita
Beckett G W	I	Salina
Brewington G W	B	Independence
Brown Henry s	B	Valley Falls
Burton Wm	H	Neosho Falls
Chamberlain J C	G	Kingman
Clark W B	H	Hazleton
Cline H J	G	Goffs
Cline Levi	G	Goffs
Cornis John	A	Cherokee
Cotterell Albert	I	Morrill
Dern Isaac N	A	Carntyne
Douglas John c	I	Topeka
Edmunds E	H	Cherryvale
Elston J W		Hutchinson
Evans Henry	G	Topeka
Fisher J S c	H	Cedarvale
Flory A M		Emporia
Forgey A J	B	Salina
Franklin J T s m	A	Topeka
Galloway J N	C	Melville
Gandy Adam c	K	Topeka
Gill J H	H	Hutchinson
Guthrie John capt	D	Topeka
Hardesty John	C	Dodge City
Haskell L R	K	New Albany
Hill B B	F	Melvern
Hitchens W H	D	Burlington
Horine H	B	Great Bend
Kinsey W A	A	Troy
Kreller J G c	I	Coffeyville
Leonard J H	D	Topeka
Martin H	B	Topeka
McNamar J V c	A	Hiawatha
Marling H T	B	Topeka
McCorkle G R	C	Columbus
Navell David	A	Alma
Preston F M	A	Beulah
Price Lewis s	H	Cascade
Rader W H H lt	G	Ford City
Robinson John s	F	Meriden
Rodgers T lt	B	Topeka
Roof D	B	Iola
Rooney John	K	Phillipsburg
Ross James	K	Howard
Ryan J C	A	Independence
Shiras Chas	A	Salina
Skinner A J s	H	Burlingame
Snowberger D	F	Oswego
Stacey A G	E	Topeka
Thomas W F	B	N Topeka
Thomas E A	G	Strong City
Tilton D M s	G	McPherson
Voorhees A L c	B	Russell
Wallace B L		Iola
White R	A	McCune
White Allen	G	Meriden
Winters I R	B	Caldwell
Young Thomas c	H	Cedarvale
Young Razel	E	Strong City
Young M M	E	Strong City

FORTY-SEVENTH REGIMENT INFANTRY,

THREE YEARS VETERANS.

Colonels—J. R. Slack, J. A. McLaughlin.

Name	Co.	Residence
Adams J H s	E	Baker
Adams Henry c	E	Baker
Baer Dan	B	Blue Rapids
Baker Josiah	D	Edna
Bigby J J	H	Delphos
Bishop Jacob	K	St John
Bowen A A c	E	Ellis
Breckenridge T W s	A	Louisburg
Brothers E W	C	Climax
Brown J H s	I	Geuda Springs
Burgess J C	I	Canton
Calvert J W	K	Neosho Rapids
Campbell Wm 'lt	B	Lawrence
Carey Peter lt	K	Burton
Davis G W c	E	Willis
Davis J T M	E	Augusta
Edwards Wm	D	McCune
Eaus J R	E	Whiting
Evans J W s	K	Mound Valley
Fooshe Gabriel	E	Grand Summit
Gashorn Wm	F	Junction
Grider A	B	Kansas City Mo
Hatfield S	D	Popcorn
Heath Sencea c	E	Atchison
Hopkins James	K	Douglas
Houser David	I	Oxford
Humes Geo	C	Bunker Hill
Jones Wm	A	Glenn
Lenhart Joseph s	C	Fawn Creek
Lines Jacob s	I	Kingman
Mabbitt T J	D	Auburn
Madison Amos	A	Independence
Malcomb Isaac		Barnard
Manning W Z	H	Waterloo
Mayne W B	K	Howard
McKinsey J A lt	K	El Dorado
McLaughlin J A col		Topeka
Mohn John	F	Laura
Montgomery J P	K	Douglas
Moore Philip s	B	Carmel
Moore Orton o	A	Wilson
Pope W A	G	Cherryvale
Rager John	B	Kingman
Reece L C c	E	Ward
Riley Geo	G	Hamilton
Sanders R M	K	Parksville
Siling Tielman J capt	D	Rockville
Sayer B F	B	Harper
Smith B C	H	Sedgwick
Smith O H	G	Wichita
Smith H H	F	Topeka
Suffield D T	G	Marion
Tate L A	A	Palmer
Thompson J W	H	Morgansville
Truby A	E	Glen Elder
Van Buskink B F	K	Mound City
Wade Geo G		LaCrosse
Warford John c	K	Fall River
Washburn W E	I	Media
Wantz J J	B	Yates Center
Weidner D	I	Pike
Whitsel H	B	Oxford
Wire Andrew	H	Quenemo
Wise W M s	F	Centropolis
Yantis John	E	Glen Elder
Young Jesse	D	Kingman

Cols. Norman Eddy, E. J. Wood, Newton
Bingham.

Attman Henry	C	Newton
Ady L L	H	Cimarron
Amos W H	K	Keelville
Biddle Thos c	B	Clyde
Bonman S c	G	McPherson
Bradford E D	I	Ophir
Brand N S lt	C	Olathe
Bresette E J	E	Rossville
Baran A J	K	Seneca
Bassett H E	I	Williamsburg
Campbell R E	K	Xenia or Havana
Clelan S W	D	Alma
Cary R S	G	* Cawker City
Crouch C P g	A	Rantoul
Crazan C W	D	Kirwin
Curtis Chancey	A	Rantoul
Davis Caleb	C	Haverhill
Deppin J N	F	Kirwin
Dutch Peter s	H	Burdgeville
Evans A E s	F	Farlinville
Funk Adam	I	Cherryvale
Gosport Jackson	A	Bulls City
Gouyer Andrew	F	Grenola
Graveldinger P c	H	Hanover
Greene A H capt	D	Winfield
Grey H W s	G	Muscotah
Harris Robt	C	Cambridge
Hand S R c	K	Independence
Hetzel M J	D	Offerle
Irwin James	A	Lone Elm
Jacobs Michael	I	Verbeck
Johnston W F	E	Rossville
Keplinger J H	A	Marion
Kilpatrick Azariah	E	Moline
Laning S surg		Kingman
Lantz Isaac	I	Lane
Leatherman W J	K	Junction City
Libbie E B	H	Elk City
Lord J H	I	Williamsburg
Luddy A J	K	Conklin
McBroom H J	C	Spearville
Metcalf Joel		Parsons
Miles Wm S	D	New Salem
Mow Wiley	C	Emporia
Murphy Asa	K	Haverhill
Neddo John	E	Rossville
Owens Squire	C	LaBette
Paul Joseph	D	Scandia
Pfaff Daniel	I	LaBette
Pidge Ed	F	Salina
Pixler Peter	I	Fowler
Preston L Z	B	Scottsville
Replogle J W	E	Kansas City
Robinson Wm	D	Great Bend
Sayler Benj	K	Clyde
Schaick J G c	D	Lawrence
Schaubel Gotleib capt	H	Fancy Creek
Shank Fred	G	Wall Street
Sheldon S F	F	Bronson
Silvers F M	A	Traer
Squiers E V o-s	D	Ft Scott
Stoops A s	C	Burlingame
Swartz J B	I	Cherryvale
Tarbell W L	I	Corbit
Thomas Joseph	A	Harper
Thomas J H	K	Kirwin
Tobias Mahlon		Salina
Walters J T	K	Junction City

Waymire Jacob	A	Melrose
Waymire N	K	Melrose
Weathers N C c	K	Chase
Weist H	D	Richmond
Wickama W A	B	Salina
Willard Dennis	C	Eldorado
Wilson W S	H	Joplin
Wight G W c	G	Burlingame
Work W W	D	Erie

FORTY-NINTH REGIMENT INFANTRY, THREE YEARS VETERAN.

Cols. John W. Ray, James Keigwin, James Leeper.

Amey Geo W	F	Buffalo
Andrews J M s	G	Neosho Falls
Anderson T N	K	Fall River
Armstrong C	F	Holton
Ball D C m		Berlin
Boaz E C		Ft Scott
Cousins John	B	Chanute
Covert J H	D	Eldorado
DeVore P F	C	Martin
Dillino R F lt	B	Hutchinson
Dillon Thos s	D	Edna
Dodd Joseph s	C	Burrton
Dotson B s	F	Great Bend
Gilbert M W	F	Wilmot
Grider A	B	Kansas City Mo
Hensly G W	E	Twin Creek
Hosea T M	D	Marion
Hunter E C	C	Kingman
Jones Elbert c	D	Halstead
Kellems R	H	Fawn Creek
La Fou N capt	K	Wilsey
Lee Josephus	B	Peabody
Likes Daniel	K	Rochester
Martin J E	C	Turin
McCandless E P	D	Grenola
Mills Henry	A	Canton
Moore Sol c	G	Rest
Niles E P	E	Kirwin
Pendley S F s	K	Wall Street
Pound L C s	B	Canton
Ransom Isaac	C	Pleasanton
Reed John W s	D	Clay Center
Reed W T	D'	Clay Center
Robertson W F s	B	Hiawatha
Smith G W s	C	Milan
Smith W B	C	Dodge City
Strange J S o-s	K	Lincoln
Stutsman T A	B	Lincolnville
Thayer C	K	Clifford
Thompson M H		Marion
Vandever C c	F	Golden Belt
Westerman W H	A	Topeka
Wilson J W c	B	LeLoup
Worthington E R	K	Densmore
Wroughtin W H	D	Wichita

FIFTIETH REGIMENT INFANTRY, THREE YEARS VETERANS.

Colonels—C. L. Dunham, S. T. Wells.

Akens Wm	K'	Almena
Anderson Amos	C	Range
Anderson J M capt	C	Salina
Avel Wm	I	Glasco
Blalock A J s		Fredonia
Bledso P F	F	Bronson
Bowers Chas	A	Fredonia
Bright J G c	H	Wichita

Name	Co.	Residence
Briner Andrew	A	Cuba
Brobst Henry	F	Minneapolis
Brown D G	G	LaBette City
Burrell A J capt	G	Arkansas City
Burt II H	F	Bennington
Butler J M c	D	Dandy
Davis F M	K	Lane
Denning B	E	Verbeck
Duncan C B	A	Leavenworth
Durand A M asst surg		Mt Hope
Emery Stephen	B	Ladore
Erwin Robt	G	Paola
Finley W M	B	Topeka
Flack W C surg		Enterprise or Council Grove
Gardner J A	F	Buffalo
Godfrey James s	C	Towanda
Gwin J M c	D	Howard
Hubbard James	A	Iall
D R Kindred	G	South Center
Luther Frank	E	Cherryvale
Mannel J K	H	Kinsley
Mattock J R s	C	Farlington
McCoy M capt	A	Cleveland
McDowell Wm	F	Monrovia
Moore Jonathan s	B	Smith Center
Moore Jacob	B	Smith Center
Morris Hilton	D	Howard
Neal A H	I	Frankfort
Newby J S	Ii	Metz
Nikirk W C capt	D	Elk City
Newkirk J C c s		Scandia
Owen Anderson	B	Cascade
Proctor Geo W	E	Matfield Green
Ray John	G	Harper
Richardson E	H	McLouth
Robins R	C	Clyde
Rucker S M	A	Spring Side
Scott J capt	II	Hutchinson
Scott D	A	North Topeka
Smith L W	K	Topeka
Speer A G 1st lt	G	Yates Center
Tarr J H P	F	Parsons
Thomas James	G	Muscotah
Thompson D A L	B	North Topeka
Watt James o s	D	Morrill
Wood Calvin c	F	Pleasanton,

FIFTY-FIRST REGIMENT INFANTRY, THREE YEARS, VETERAN.

Cols. A. D. Streight, David A. McHolland Wm. N. Denny.

Name	Co.	Residence
Adair Wm 1st lt	A	Burlington
Adams G H	C	Junction City
Ashby James c	E	Urbana
Back E S s	G	Reading
Bates J N	C	Salem
Booker T H	H	Reece
Booker Levi H lt	H	Eureka
Cooper Henry	A	Hallowell
Corn James	B	Marion
Cox John S	II	Mound Valley
Cox I H	K	Parsons
Dennis R A	B	Oak Valley
Dunn W H 1st lt	H	Topeka
Eads James	D	Elmdale
Fossett R c	F	Kansas City Mo
Ferguson K	B	Greeley
Gilbert W F c	C	Oswego
Givens J A capt	A	Topeka
Gwin J A	B	Walnut
Haney Ephraim	B	Scandia

Name	Co.	Place
Harlan John	A	Burlington
Harper W W s	E	Mound Valley
Harrington J H	B	Lucerne
Harrison James	C	Concordia
Helms James s	B	Metz
Henderson H C	F	Mulvane
Henney Geo	B	Scandia
Hensley James	D	Burden
Humphrey R F	B	Wichita
Jelf W H s	C	Cloverdale
Johnson W W c	E	Wichita
Justice W	E	Melvern
Lewis W R capt	B	Axtell
Mast Amos	C	Columbus
Mayes E C	K	Galesburg
McClure J H m	E	Girard
McClure W P capt	H	Thompsonville
McClure C N s	H	Wall Street
McGrew Jackson	F	Colony
Moore H C	A	Silver Lake
Moore B F	K	Ellinwood
Morgan T J 1st s	F	Fall River
Morris Mason	A	Leon
Mowbray M C	F	Willis
Myers A	B	Hutchinson
Neff John	A	Augusta
Noles John T	E	Baldwin
Paddock T H	H	Wall Street
Parr W P asst surg		Emporia
Parkhurst W T	A	Como
Polsom Wm	K	North Topeka
Rhodes G W	I	Wauneta
Rodman J H s	D	Moline
Ross Henry	F	Atchison
Scritchfield O S	E	Westmoreland
Sergeant A W s	I	Lyndon
Sharpe E E 1st lt	D	Salina
Shambaugh J	D	Whiting
Sherman E A c	B	North Topeka
Shoemaker J F	H	Hallowell
Smith B F c	B	Wakeman
Staton J	B	Neodesha
Stafford Geo	F	Iola
Stuckey Fred	H	Emporia
Summers W C	C	Chase
Templin R T	C	Ida
Terrill S F	E	Altamont
Taylor Daniel	K	Gaylord
Thomas J H		Kirwin
Todd J H	A	Wichita
Tout J W c	C	Grenola
Trimble J R c	I	Cool
Tudor W F	G	Meriden
Turner W	F	Corvallis
Thoroughman W W	B	Yates Center
Vincent J B	H	Nickerson
Walker J	G	Cheney
Ward W P	A	Ft Scott
Waugh V S	E	Sedgewick

FIFTY SECOND REGIMENT INFANTRY, THREE YEARS VETERANS.

Colonels—James M. Smith, Edward H. Wolfe, Zalmon S. Main.

Name	Co.	Place
Armstrong T	B	Gibson
Barber M L s	H	Abilene
Barber Moses lt	H	Dodge City
Benton J R	H	Burden
Benton H	H	Tisdale
Bunton E	C	LeRoy
Chitwood J M		Harper

Coffey H M c	K	White Rock
Collier J B	A	Haddam
Cooper Sterling	K	Wauneta
Cox W A J	D	Westphalia
Davis James	B	Canton
Ellis J W	F	Osage Mission
Eugene Hugh	A	Montana
Finley W M	A	Topeka
Ford Irwin s	B	Albion
Frost E	B	Cherryvale
Gardner J A	B	Buffalo
Guard Mahlon c	D	Beloit
Hanover J A	H	Chanute
Hawley W s	A	Conway Springs
Heizer J E c	K	Ness City
Hesson John c	K	Osawkee
Homer W	D	Caldwell
Jaques A C	A	Sidney
Marshall T K	I	Garnett
Mattocks E capt	C	Atchison
McKee John	B	Dexter
McJohn	B	Winfield
McMahan O C s	B	Toronto
Owen Albert capt	A	Meriden
Pate Ed c	C	Burdea
Proctor John	C	Burrton
Richardson W W s	I	Twin Falls
Richardson W H	H	Clyde
Sample W D	B	Canton
Sherman A H	I	Yates Center
Skinner H	I	Haskell
Spencer W L	K	Oxford
Spencer S M	K	Oxford
Spencer W S	K	Sedan
Stewart G W s	G	New Albany
Swift C	D	Aubrey
Tevis J M capt	K	Topeka
Vilott G S s	H	Mankato

FIFTY-THIRD REGIMENT INFANTRY, THREE YEARS AND VETERAN.

Cols. W. Q. Gresham, William Jones, Warner L. Vestal.

Anderson J W		South Haven
Austin J M lt	B	Culver
Aumon Peter	F	Baxter Springs
Belveale Seth	A	Rosalind
Beaver Perry	A	New Church
Black Harrison	A	Burlingame
Chapman J B	D	Fountain
Davis P R	F	Topeka
Dolman John		North Topek
Donnell W S	K	Augusta
Dalton Sam'l	I	Topeka
Esslinger F G	B	Wilson
Fabrique A H maj		Wichita
Funk A B c	B	Strawn
Garr J J	K	Cherryvale
Goff David s	H	Oswego
Gould W K	K	Plainville
Green J M	E	Parsons
Hahn J N	E	Guilford
Hockman L S s	C	Eureka
Jenkins Joseph	K	Hortenburg
Kinnaman H		Brush Creek
Kessler Jacob	A	Neosho Falls
Knight David c	K	Blaine
Kintner T B c	B	Fellsbur
Lafferty L D	K	Olivet
Lewis Clinton capt	H	Hunnewell

Name	Co.	Residence
Lonsdale G W	C	Centralia
Loughmiller A J s	D	Prescott
Matthews N lt	I	Wamego
McDaniel Jacob		Capioma
McKnight S	C	Gatesville
Michael John	F	Cherryvale
Murphy W T	K	Cora
Newkirk J	I	Erie
Park H H	K	Winfield
Powell J B c	F	Mortimer
Prather B F	A	Havana
Ragan W W capt	A	Oswego
Reginald N	G	•Peterton
Ricketts J J	D	Saratoga
Riley G W		Urbana
Ryan H C	I	Independence
Sage G W	K	Montana
Shannon T N	G	Sylvan Grove
Shoemaker J F	C	Hallowell
Shuyler J S	G	Nickerson
Summers Geo	B	Cheney
Taylor J A	H	Yates Center
Townsend J F capt	C	Garnett
Wendell A	B	Roy
Woolf A M	I	Andover

FIFTY FOURTH INFANFRY 3 MONTHS' SERVICE.

Cols. John L. Mansfield, David Garland Rose.

FIFTY FOURTH INFANTRY, ONE YEARS' SERVICE.

Col. Fielding Mansfield.

Name	Co.	Residence
Bellas C W	B	Burlington
Bradbury James	C	Purity
Brown W H	A	Cicero
Butcher Levi	D	Mound City
Butt Geo	K	Yates Center
Critchfall J N s	H	Arkansas City
Custer J N	E	Peru
Davis Alonzo s	I	Concordia
Davis Wm m	I	Abilene
Eby A F	C	Howard
Flora James	D	Clifton
Fortune L F	K	Zeandale
Frankey C	I	Great Bend
Graham R L	E	Quenemo
Harshman E J	G	LaCygne
Hart Wm lt		Parsons
High I H c	E	Milan
Houston W W	A	Tabor
Hudson John	E	Chetopa
Hunt S H	A	Wellsville
Hurst Jacob	K	Blue Mound
Johnson L W s	B	Belle Plains
Lawson Thos	D	Oswego
Logan D M capt	F	Ft Scott
Lowe Benj F	K	Keene
Loyd G R	K	Sedan
Manning M		Carlyle
McHugh C W	E	Sedan
McKee J G s	F	Farlington
Myers James	I	Coffeyville
McNeill G H	H	Arkansas City
Murphy F A	C	Wabaunsee
Newman Leroy	I	Verdigrie
Scott G C lt	E	Toogana
Sharp Rob't	F	Norwood
Shelley H	H	Atwood
Smith Asa	I	Girard

Strahan S P lt	G	Bea
Swan L D	B	Walnut
Vance Amos	C	Havensville
Walker W F	I	Elk City
Warner J c	H	Morrill
Wilson Scott	G	Arkansas City
Wire N S s	G	Kedron
Wood Joseph	H	Winfield

FIFTY-FIFTH INFANTRY, THREE MONTHS SERVICE.

Lt. Col. John R. Mahan.

Berger Philip	I	Neutral
Brown Kelsey	H	Salina
Cain Wm	K	Elk City
Clark F A	K	Yates Center
Gentry M H	K	LeRoy
Gilbert D	H	Severy
Gill S E	E	Pipe Creek
Grace Geo	H	Carthage
Kerr James J	F	Junction City
Layton J M	G	Chetopa
LeMasters John	H	Sterling
Lemon J W	E	Kirwin
Stalnaker W H	B	Kansas City Mo
Starr J S s		Neosho Rapids
Stone E P	G	Norton
Trower G W	G	Winchester
Vestal J C s	H	Eldorado
Wade G A	K	Mortimer
Ward E C	H	Iola
Wilson M	D	Milford

Fifty-sixth Regiment Indiana Infantry was authorized, but not completed; the men enlisted for it were consolidated with the Fifty-second Regiment.

FIFTY-SEVENTH INFANTRY, 3 YEARS AND VETERANS.

Colonels, J. W. T. McMullen, Cyrus C. Hines, Geo. W. Leonard, Willis Blanch and John S. McGraw.

Allison Robert capt	A	Winfield
Allison W M	A	Wellington
Baker D P	K	Fredonia
Baker J S	G	Morantown
Bannon T J	C	Neodesha
Bartlow O W	A	Lyle
Barnes E	F	N Topeka
Boughman T K Osage Misison or Walnut		
Bean Thomas	K	Burlington
Bohrer R J s	I	Cawker City
Brown N c	F	Baldwin
Cabbage A	D	Antrim
Campbell J J sutler		Chetopa
Childers W	E	Long Island
Chance Asa c	H	Middleton
Commons D M	C	Thayer
Dick L F 1 s	H	Parsons
Duterow P A	C	Cloverdale
Farl Isaac T capt	A	Eskridge
Ellis Henry	G	Byron
Falls J W capt	E	Altoona
Fisk G O	A	Madison
Goodwin Jacob	G	Pretty Prairie
Gordon Joseph	E	Yates Center
Hall J W	G	Beloit
Hart R W c	D	Parsons

Name	Co.	Residence
Harvey J M 1 s	C	Topeka
Horn L S 1 lt	H	Mankato
Harrod H s	H	Winfield
Jewell J	K	Castleton
Jones Harry assist surg		Junction City
Keenan Oscar	K	Lyndon
Loser Wm	E	Colnmbus
McReynolds J W	G	Columbus
Mills Levi	H	Dunlap
Moore B F s	K	Ellinwood
Murphy F A	C	St George
Newport J	E	Monmouth
Nicodemus J	F	Peabody
Need John	F	Andrew
Norris G G s	I	South Haven
Parrish A	A	Blue Mound
Phillips E F s	H	Lawrence
Preble H O S	H	Paradise
Seagraves W J	G	Lerado
Shidlers H B	K	Topeka
Shiyers R	F	Clay Center
Shivers W	F	Wakefield
Shook Jer'e	I	Columbus
Small F F	H	Winfield
Smith Arioch	H	Dresden
Sims J S	H	Topeka
Stizetman	K	Ackerland
Thomas M c	G	Nickerson
Thorne J W	K	Abilene
Van Dyke M A		Mule Creek or Little River
Vanzandt W W	A	Athelstone
White H S	C	Gaylord
Wintermote J	C	Cherryvale or Neodesha
Wright J C	O	Sedgewick

FIFTY-EIGHTH INFANTRY—THREE YEAR AND VETERANS.

Colonels, Henry M. Carr, Geo. P. Buell.

Name	Co.	Residence
Agee W A	D	Jetmore
Anderson J T c	F	Mound Valley
Bass Jacob	C	Clay Center
Bell C G	I	Richland
Binkley Calvin c	C	Clay Center
Brenter J B	E	Walton
Brewster John	D	Hallowell or Oswego
Brenton Henry	G	Farmersburg
Bryant A M q m sgt		Gettysburg
Crozier J G	C	Peabody
David Jacob c	B	St John
Ellers J W	D	Osage Mission
Emerson J E	G	Russell
Essex, T J	F	Burlington
Everett J A	H	Dennis
Gray C M G	I	Chanute
Hadlock D M 1st lt	C	Bennington
Hamilton Aaron	I	Marion Center
Hedrick I T	B	Eldridge
Hopkins J A	F	Opolis
Housley Mack	H	Cedarvale
Hughes H	E	Harveysville
Hughes Robt	F	Kingman
Jay Moses s	B	Wichita
Kirk V T	K	Oswego
Knight Isaac	A	Burden
Lawrence S	D	Chetopa
Ledgerwood S	E	Neosho Falls
Lynch R F	G	Bunker Hill
Martin S P	G	Independence
Martin T R	G	Independence
Martin L G	G	Howard

Mason L C capt	F	Independence
Mason M B	D	Parsons
McPaul M V	D	Neodesha
Mendell M C	D	Parsons
Miller James	G	Vansburg
Morgan R W	B	Douglas
McReynolds J T	C	Mound City
Niles J Q	F	Rochester
Potts Joseph	G	Great Bend
Rice F A	D	Lyons
Rodarmel James	E	Farmersburg
Sealock J R	E	Newton
Simpson J W	G	Belle Plaine
Sparks J F c	H	Hallowell
Tanquary D	C	Columbus
Traylor M W	H	Emporia
Underwood H H	H	Pleasant Plains
Utley S F 1st lt	K	Waterloo
Wilson J	K	Wichita
Wilson W M	B	Girard

FIFTY-NINTH INFANTRY, 3 YEARS AND VETERANS.

Colonels—Jesse I Alexander, Jeff K. Scott and Thomas A. McNaught.

Alburn J H	K	Florence
Andrew W W	D	Hollenburg
Bales A H	H	Washington
Beem Wm	D	New Albany
Boice J C W m	E	Kansas City Mo
Bryant J B	B	Longton
Buckner John	C	Axtell
Byrum J R	A	Dora
Cantwell S	H	Wilson
Cassida Thos	A	Fontana
rider M	G	McPherson
Critchfield W G	G	Osborne
Deweese W H q m s	K	Wamego
Dome Chas H	K	Wichita
Evans Sevier	D	Densmore
Fisens Jacob	A	Paw Paw
Ford L S	C	Independence
Fiouff T	B	Strong City
Geyen N	D	Clyde
Grass John D	G	Parsons
Hammer W T	D	Altamont
Hamlin G H c	G	Fort Scott
Hinline Peter	F	Salem
Hill W N	E	Severy
Hoover P C	C	Parsons
Johnson John		Salina
Knapp G W unassigned		Douglas
Lehman O	C	Xenia
Masters L R	B	Garden Plains
McBride Robt	A	Mapleton
Middleton A W	A	Thayer
Milan J S	A	Purdy
Newman G W	G	Sterling
Orner Theo F capt	I	Topeka
Peter Simon	F	Newton
Pop John	C	Atwood
Pracky Moses	C	Manhattan
Redfield J D	F	Morehead
Rariden M D s	D	McPherson
Rehstock S S	G	Newton
Richards John	E	Parsons
Rodenburger P	K	Star Valley
Shidler H	G	Monmouth
Smith W H	D	Havana
Smock W L	E	Talmo

Stanley S O	C	Minneapolis,
Starrett W H	F	Columbus
Stroud Jesse	F	Morehead
Sutherland J M adj		Leavenworth
Tipton Josah	G	McPherson
Toler A J	C	Baxter Springs
Tyner OP	G	Tannehill
Van Lieu J A	D	Spring Creek
Williamson A	G	Wellington
Wilson Andrew c	B	Anthony
Winn Thos	K	Kiowa
Winters A H	A	Concordia
Winters W J	A	Concordia
Young Alex	E	Augusta

SIXTIETH INFANTRY, THREE YEARS AND VETERAN.

Cols. Richard Owen, Augustus Goelzer.

Adams W R	D	Fredonia
Bectold Fred	D	Tapley
Bellice David	B	Oak Hill
Bowman J M c	H	Dennis
Canette Philis	D	Zurich
Carter Ivan	K	Rantoul
Cook J G	H	Rosalia
Cox Levi	H	Arcadia
Creek J H	B	Harper
Cunningham E	I	Urbana
Davis J	K	Osage City
Downing H P capt	H	Rosalia
Garten J H c	B	Oswego
Givens W B capt	K	Leavenworth
Hamilton T E	D	Columbus
Hartington M	H	Greeley
McClure T N	K	North Topeka
Moyer Henry	D	Wetmore
Osman Philip	I	Sunnyvale
Petty Eli J	I	Hutchinson
Rickstraw W H	D	Arispie
Settles N D	K	Belleville

Sixty-first, Second Irish Regiment was not organized. The enlisted men and a few of the officers were transferred to the Thirty-fifth Regiment, Infantry.

Sixty second Regiment was only partly organized when it was consolidated with the Fifty-third Infantry Regiment.

SIXTY THIRD REGIMENT, INFANTRY, THREE YEARS VETERANS.

Colonels—John S. Williams, James Mc-Manomy, Israel N. Stiles.

Allen G W	G	Cherokee
Ashley Alonzo	A	Lenexa
Aughe D T capt	I	Erie
Baker A T	H	Cherryvale
Baker Isaac	H	Altamont
Basey W A	D	Columbus
Basey J. M.	E	Columbus
Blair J	H	Saltville
Bool L D.	E	Humboldt
Brown David l	G	Wakarusa
Burch Milton	I	Auburn
Caldwell W W	E	Americus
Cleaghorn T H	I	Longton
Cory W H	C	Rambelt

Coffman Geo capt	K	Valencia
Coffman John	K	Silver Lake
Cranmer James	A	Logan
Catt John	D	Ft Scott
Dawson Holt	G	Osage City
De Bruler J N	C	Independence
Dunkerly S qm	B	Madison
Dunfee J W s	G	Guilford
Edwards Wesley	I	Cimarron
Fogleman J M	I	Mound Valley
Gates S F	H	Fall River
Hansom M	I	Adams Peak
Hardesty W H	F	Floral
Hardy W R	B	Eureka
Hathway F M	E	Dexter
Henderson W F capt	C	Erie
Hiestand I B	B	Elk Falls
Howdy Shell T c	C	Neodesha
Hutton Thos	H	Argonia
Johnston J S	D	Diamond Springs
Keller C P	D	Fall River
Knisely W B	E	Lansing
Leatherman A c	G	Leon
Long C W	E	Pittsburg
Ludlow James H s	B	Crestline
Ludlow John S	B	Crestline
McAfee H	E	Grafton
McCloud C F c		Sutphen Mills
McManomy Nash	D	Mayfield
Myers Hiram s	C	Matthewson
Neidigh F M c	I	Chetopa
Peak F M	B	Arkansas City
Pennell Wm	E	Russell
Rains John	B	Concordia
Riley Thos	H	Eureka
Riley W B s	C	Baxter Springs
Sanders W N	K	Leon
Schell Wm	C	Coyville
Shaff Joseph s	H	Cloverdale
Shannon D W c	C	Girard
Shepard Wm c	D	Spearville
Sluder G W	F	Kingston
Storms Jacob	H	Le Roy
Tague John	C	Columbus
Turner S P c	K	Star
Wade B	F	Fall River
Webb Harris c	A	Lenore
White W F	F	Richland
Willey W W	K	Clay Center

SIXTY FOURTH, INDIANA INFANTRY—Not organized.

SIXTY FIFTH REGIMENT INFANTRY, THREE YEARS.

Colonels—John W. Foster, Thos Johnson, John W. Hammond.

Admire J V capt	E	Osage City
Barnett W O	D	Wellington
Boyden J A	D	Towanda
Carey G W capt	D	North Topeka
Cheppel J L	K	Walton
French P J	D	Wyandotte
Galbreath S A c	B	Eldridge
Huston J L	A	Dexter
Lloyd S B 1st s	I	Emporia
Mack J R	F	Olivet
Mansell W B	H	Cawker City
Marmaduke J A	I	Elk City

Robrson E B c	I	Menoken
St Clair J F	F	Empire City
Stephen s W F s	B	Eldridge
Stucker Joseph c	I	Syuth Center
Swaney A D	F	Mulvane
Trainer John	C	Scandia
Tyler W J	I	LaCygne
Wise A H	I	Topeka

SIXTY-SIXTH REGIMENT INFANTRY, THREE YEARS.

Cols. Lew Wallace, D. C. Anthony, Roger Martin.

Adams J W	H	Newton
Arnold E W	C	Stockton
Atkinson Thos	D	Harrisonville
Baxter Hectable capt A		James' Crossing
Brown Wm	A	Lorne
Burris J T	G	Golden Belt
Chambers Jesse lt	A	Humboldt
Collings K H	K	Havensville
Conrad S I 1st s	C	Mound Valley
Cromer J P	H	Wellington
Denny S P	B	Williamstown
Epperson W T	G	Wyandotte
Ferguston N c	K	Chautauqua
Gibbons James c	F	Sweet Home
Gibson Robt	H	Winfield
Glover W M	B	Parsons
Gould R H s	A	Elm Valley
Griggs Lyman	D	Olivet
Hammersly M G c	A	Elm Valley
Hardin W C	G	Bridge
Herron J A	F	Eskridge
Hobson R H	D	Clear Water
Hugh J L	A	Lane
Hunter W H c	B	Parsons
Hurst Besale	C	Kinsley
Jean G W	A	Galena
Johnston W H	K	Center Ridge
Livengood W J	E	Topeka
Lynn S W c	A	Mortimer
Maxeadon Isom	D	Terrapin
Meade R J c	B	Maple City
Mellis John capt	D	Paola
Maxson Isom	D	Terrapin
Marander T H	F	Cora
Miller Philip	K	Salina
Monaghan D	A	Mortimer
Phipps J A	E	Olathe
Ranson J A	H	Osage City
Sawtell Ira	A	Montana
Spellman S	K	Salina
Standeford N	B	Peterton
Stewart R P c	H	Bloomington Neb
Stratton G D lt	B	Walton
Taylor G W	B	Dexter
Thompson B T c	F	Cloverdale
Toler Jesse	C	Kinsley
Walker A R lt	A	Onaga
Wallace J A	E	Galesburg
Winslow J W	F	Stuart

SIXTY-SEVENTH REGIMENT INFANTRY, THREE YEARS.

Col. Frank Emerson.

Bartup Jesse c	G	Kansas City
Bowman J D	A	Sedan
Brown W H s	A	Kinsley
Brown Jacob	K	Arnold

Bunton W S	G	Vining
Burton G	H	Olivet
Crane J M	G	Leonardsville
Cristler J A s	I	LaCygne
Draper Eli	D	Farlington
Friedly W W lt	I	Winfield or West Plains
Findley G M	K	Coyville
Hornaday	K	Cherokee
Hostetter B F	H	Farlinville
Johnson W S	A	Leon
Johnson John	A	Urbana
Lenning John	D	Arkansas City
Lloyd W J	D	Eskridge
Love Alex	E	Tonganoxie
Luckey Willis	D	Glen Elder
Meier James	C	North Topeka
Metcalf R	G	Thayer
Miller J H	H	Ottawa
Parish Gabriel	D	Otto
Rhoades A J		Severy
Robinson Gab'l	K	Arkansas City
Rutherford J	D	Otto
Smith J T	E	Reno Center
Snyder Levi	D	Thayer
Thompson J W	G	Morganville
Young A J	A	Ottawa

SIXTY EIGHTH REGIMENT INFANTRY, THREE YEARS.

Cols. Edward A. King, John S. Scobey, Harvey J. Espy.

Arnold O A	D	Quenemo
Arnold W S	K	Quenemo
Austin S L	K	East Wolf
Bird W F s	A	Mound Valley
Castor Benj	F	Wichita
Childers Jesse	I	Wellington
Clark James W	C	Council Grove
Davis T C c	I	Delphos
Dawson J H s	K	Quenemo
Farmer J A c	H	Marion
Gibbs T W	E	Cherryvale
Hessler Frank	A	Barry
Howell G W	H	Bross
Howell C W	I	Smith Center
Kibby M H 1st lt	C	Milierton
Kilgore E c	H	Abilene
Leaswell T D	B	Neosho Falls
Lewis E	C	Lincoln
McCready S s	G	Marion
McCready J A c	G	Florence
McGlin James	C	Fredonia
McShane Frank c	A	Gardiner
Moore Marcus	E	West Cedar
Neff Rudolph s	E	Glen Elder
Ploughe N T m	D	Thompsonville
Pappino S C	D	Chanute
Powers Joseph	I	Coffeyville
Reed Barnett	H	Paola
Shaw Wilson	B	Winfield
Shuman T S	K	Glen Elder
Simpson J H	I	Sterling
Smith G W	C	Sterling
Smith James	E	Gale
Smith John	E	Gale
Stevenson W T c	K	Humboldt
Thackery S	F	Glasco
Thackery S L	F	Manhattan
Thompson J W c	I	Farlinville
Tower A W	K	Galva
Vanlaudigham L T	H	Harper

VanSchoiack J G	B	Ottawa
Wiley A J	A	Pomeroy
Winkleman J K	F	Hanover
Yates T B	G	McPherson
Zook James	E	Holton

SIXTY-NINTH REGIMENT, INFANTRY, THREE YEARS.

Colonels—Wm A. Bickel, T. W. Bennett.

Adamson S R s	D	Walnut
Alason A	K	Lincoln
Bartholomew S	C	Clinton
Brewer Thomas	C	Clinton
Byers W F	B	East Wolf
Callahan J W	I	Ida
Coffield E	A	Delphos
Coggeshall Allen	E	Altoona
Coggeshall N B lt	E	Chelsea
Ebenstein C F	B	Baxter Springs
Farmer William	E	Hector
Farmer J S s	H	Baileyville
Flinn Frank	C	Frankfort
Freeman A B	E	Fall River
Fulgrum T E c	F	Hays City
Gilmore W L	K	Monroe
Harder R H	B	Paola
Hartley J F	I	Baxter Springs
Hines W C lt	B	Cedarvale
Hoober J B	I	Independence
Hollings A P	D	Mankato
Hunt H C	D	Newton
Kimmell D c	H	Spearville
Kimbraugh D	E	Moline
Little W T	F	Rosedale
L'oyd G W	D	Cottonwood Falls
Mackey Gilbert	C	Altoona
Macy A C	D	Hobart
Marshall I E	F	Hutchinson
Potter Sidney	F	North Topeka
Priest Frank	K	Shady Bend
Qnigly A R	E	Elk City
Rudd Adam	D	Colorado
Scott A M	C	Wellington
Slinger A J 1st lt	I	Wichita
VanWinkle R R	H	Belleville
Way J S 1st lt	C	Independence
Williams A	B	Oswego
Wiseman J H	A	Wamego
Woody C M	A	Clifton

SEVENTIETH REGIMENT, INFANTRY, THREE YEARS.

Colonel, Benjamin Harrison.

Adams S E	I	Bulls City
Albright John	B	Hutchinson
Allen Gregory	D	Conway
Angleton R s	B	Eldorado
Bishop W H	I	Oberlin
Bringle J J	C	Hutchinson
Brown W S	A	Reamsville
Burgess James lt col		Topeka
Cannatsey W S	D	Iola
Claypool J W s	K	Nickerson
Coleman G A	I	Hutchinson
Collins G	F	Clifford
Crawford E C	K	Empire City
Day W W c	F	Newberne
Dixon Thos	H	Wellington

Eley T W m	H	Rock
Eoff Humphrey	B	Pratt
Evans G W	B	Runnymede
Frear James	I	Elm Valley
Fisher E R c	G	Beloit
Gordon Alex	G	Hallowell
Howland W E	K	Le Bette City
Hutchinson A W	I	Leavenworth
Hutchinson James	I	Bluff Creek
Julian James	D	Dodge City
Larry P A	A	Arkansas City
Lane Levi	D	Independence
Lee Harrison	C	Cherokee
Marcy Jacob	F	Newton
Mastin W H	C	Lawrence
McLean J C	D	Howard
McMillen G	G	Melvern
Miller Jhos c	K	Altoona
Moody Levi	I	Ft Scott
Moore J W	F	Chanute
Newby T M c	C	Smith Centre
Osborne Nicholas	C	Carbondale
Peters Joseph	G	Baxter Springs
Pray Eli T	D	Ossawatomie
Rawlings C W	G	Centerville
Rawlings Wm	G	Centerville
Reitzel J H	C	Waterville
Richardson S R c	C	Winchester
Richardson J D	C	Snow Hill
Roland W J	D	Hiattville
Sharpe Wm	C	Ward
Silvey Luther	G	Glen Elder
Smock S J	G	Winfield
Snow J F	D	Cawker City
Storms C F lt	F	Sabetha
Tansey W E capt	D	Winfield
Thomas S 1st lt	G	Chanute
Vaught Wilson	I	Iola
Walker David	F	Columbus
Wharton R T	H	Independence
Wood J W	C	Independence

SEVENTY FIRST INFANTRY, RE-ORGANIZED AS THE SIXTH CAVALRY AND VETERANS — SIXTH CAVALRY BATTALION.

Colonels—James Biddle, Courtland C. Matson.

Barrett J W Jr	I	LeRoy
Bell M	I	Hamilton
Black Joseph	B	Farlinville
Blake M	C	Kingman
Booth James c	M	Scandin
Boring J A	A	Carbondale
Capen David	L	New Kiowa
Carney D W	E	Burlington
Carter M S	A	Barnesville
Challis W B	G	Topeka
Clover Elliott	A	Glen Elder
Cook Wm	A	Ashland
Corey Geo W	E	Louisburg
Cox Geo W	G	Ridgeway
Dailey Abner	G	Eldorado
Davis S W s	I	Kingman
Davis R N c	A	Altamont
Decker Sgm'l s	F	North Cedar
Donham H L	D	Stockton
Duncan G L	D	Beloit

Fairleigh H J	com s	F	Independence
Ferguson J W		C	Constant
Fenquay J W		G	Constant
Filsow W		F	Cherryvale
Fleming W W	s	K	Paola
Fuqua Joseph		B	Grenola
Gifford E		G	Olivet
Green R F		E	Brush Creek
Griffith J M	lt	K	Emporia
Gwartner A		M	Spring Creek
Gwinn R T	com s	G	Girard
Hall Jacob		A	Moline
Hildebrand W H		L	Osage City
Hutchison Jas	s	B	Pottowattomie
Harbison G W		A	Turon
Heath T R	.	D	Lane
Henry J S		G	Monroe
Higgins D H		H	Matfield Green
Hinman Thos	s	I	Louisburg
Holtz David		K	Wichita
Hughes James		H	Abilene
Huston M		B	McPherson
Johnson C E		F	Louisville
Jones J W	c	D	Hallowell
McCall Wm		B	Quindaro
McDonald P	1st s	I	Fredonia
McHargue Thos		C	Independence
McWilliams M		C	Leavenworth
Milam J E		I	Galena
Miles John		E	Altamont
Norman Lewis		F	Alcona
Owens D C		H	Neodesha
Perkins M R		M	Ellsworth
Raugh H M		A	Carleton
Rhodes J A		A	Augusta
Risdon N S	c	D	Garnett
Sales P H		E	Girard
Sanders J H			Osawakee
Schofield J M		L	Chapman
Shaver David		A	Bashan
Sleeth James		H	Farlinville
Sleeth W H H		H	Altamont
Smith Fred		H	Republic City Neb
Smith A B	s	L	Cherryvale
Smith W S		D	Dora
Smith David		A	Cato
Steel T J	c	D	Independence
Stepp Jackson	capt	I	Independence
Stoker Ellis		K	Independence
Swisher W F		I	Morantown
Stoker John		G	Topeka
Terry W R		E	Cawker City
Thomas Wm		A	Matanzas
VanHorn A F	c	G	Keightley
Walker H S		L	Baxter Springs
Walker Smith		H	Wichita
Waite F M		A	Parsons
Wilkey H S		G	Independence
Wilkey H M		G	Independence
Work Aaron		F	North Cedar
Zenor W H		D	Medicine Lodge
Yates E N	s maj		North Topeka

SEVENTY-SECOND (MOUNTED) INFANTRY

THREE YEARS.

Col Abram O. Miller.

Adams John	J	Ottawa
Anderson R H	G	Columbus
Anderson E W	I	Wyandotte
Andrews Henry	C	Rush Center
Ash J R s	G	Wellington
Avery James J	C	Ft Scott

Baer David	G	Arkansas City
Bannan James	G	Belle Meade
Beaver Anson	I	Cedarville
Billings N K	D	Concordia
Burch Moses capt	F	Lyons
Cadwell James	F	Burrton
Calahan W H c	A	Fontana
Canutt Levi	F	Olathe
Cheney H A	H	Cuba
Clair John c	B	Parsons
Cline Thos	A	Independence
Cline David	A	Independence
Coldrudt S J s	E	Sterling
Connel T B c	E	Walnut
Council M c	D	Topeka
Curnutt H G	I	Sterling
Davis Geo W	F	Neodesha
Derby J J	C	Neosho Falls
Dickson S Y E	H	Clay Center
Dimmitt S T	F	Raymond
Drummond Jas c	I	Parsons
Etnire S M m	F	Augusta
Franklin J	I	Mound Valley
Fogle John	K	Coffeyville
Goldsberry G W	G	Columbus
Grimes T M	B	Fall River
Haines G W	F	Atchison
Hanlin W E	B	Norton
Hargraves J W	D	St Marys
Harris J L s	A	Lawrence
Haynes J F s	I	Stockton
Helms J M	H	Reece
Herr Geo c	K	Burlington
Hobaugh N	F	Arkansas City
Hooker H H	I	Polo
Hughes T E	K	Sedgewick
Hunter Samuel	G	Holton
Hunter John	G	Green
Huntsinger Isaac	A	Minneapolis
Hutchinson S R	K	Erie
Insley J N lt	E	Oskaloosa
Johnson J W	D	Iola
Johnson W L	K	Rex
Kendall James K	E	Hepler
Kent Sol c	C	Belleville
Kessee Thos	E	N Topeka
Knight J Lee s	A	Topeka
Lane A W lt	G	Burlington
Lenker W P	G	Wellington
Lewis John	D	Colony
Mayhall G W	F	N Topeka
Mayhall W	F	Cope
Medoris J W	E	Middleton
Miller E A	K	Iola
Miller G W	l	Moline
Milligan F W s	G	Circleville
Nevels S H	D	Armourdale
Nowls Moses lt	F	Allegan
Oshel Jesse	G	Neosho Falls
Poinsett W B	E	Quenemo
Ranson W H	F	Girard
Records E L	I	Peru
Rice E H	E	Blue Mound
Riley J L	D	Burdgville
Riley G F	A	Greystone
Schoonover W H s	F	Prosper
Sellers T J	C	Potterville
Shaughnessy S J	G	Hart's Mills
Shaw Wm	I	Harveyville
Southard Geo	I	Harper
Spitler Benj	A	Paola
Stafford J M	H	Clearwater
Taylor Samuel c	I	Tonganoxie

Thomas G K	E	Lenora
Toms P J		N Topeka
Vanocker M D	A	Turon
Vogan J A s	D	Forester
Walton J W	E	North Cedar
Wilson J N	H	Olathe

SEVENTY-THIRD INFANTRY, THREE YEARS SERVICE.

Colonels, Gilbert Hathaway, Alfred B Wade.

Asher I	I	Geuda Springs
Bales T C	K	Cuba
Beebe Geo M	E	Wamego
Blount J J	K	Topsy
Bowen James	K	Valley Center
Callahan A M lt	H	Topeka
Clark J M	C	Topeka
Crawford Robt	II	Iola
Cross James	B	Cowland
Cummings J E s	F	Pleasant Run
Davis H A	A	Myers Valley
Dodd Thos F C ass't surg		Altoona
Eaton Wm C capt	1	Paola
Evans Joseph R c	D	Chard
Fallis J W	H	Bernard
Fields Chambers	G	Burlington
Fisher A B	G	Ft Scott
Foust Wm c	G	Minerva
Hardner F H	A	Newton
Goddard R D	B	Onaga
Green L N	A	Burlington
Henderson J	F	Columbus
Jackson D W c	D	Longton
Jackson C D	K	Wamego
Jenners C. H.	H	Topeka
Kendall W II	C	Willis
Kendt Sol c	C	Belleville
Kennedy E A	I	Freeman
Kersey A H		Louisville
Kersey Robt 1st s	I	Louisville
Ketcham Chas	E	Range
Lansing Robert	I	St John
Masseth H	A	Piqua
McAllister Jesse	I	Hiattville
McBeebe	E	Wamego
McMasters R B	G	N Topeka
Milner G S	I	Chester, Neb
Penny N R	G	Cambridge
Richley J A capt	C	Severy
Rose J	C	Jewell City
Sanderson A E	H	Iola
Scott Oliver	F	Pittsburg
Sheeder Isaac s	G	Arkansas City
Smith A H	B	Newbern
Smith B F	D	Marshall
Smith G H	G	Marshall
Sprague J N	A	Haddam
Sprague A M	A	Kansas Center
Sprague J M	A	Ellsworth
Spencer O H	E	Monitor
Stanly R C	D	Minneapolis
Surprise H	I	Buffalo
Thompson D T s	G	Iola
Thompson Eli		Waterville
Thornton S	K	Comet
Thornton Wm	K	Comet
Vader Daniel	B	Galena
Webb D	I	Sterling
Welch James	K	Roxbury

Whitzell John	F	Neodesha
Wolford G W	G	Blue Springs
Woodford J C 1st lt	F	Paola
York James	H	Bitlertown

SEVENTY-FOURTH INFANTRY, THREE YEARS SERVICE.

Colonels— Chas. W. Chapman, Myron Baker, Thomas Morgan.

Abbott A V	A	Havensville
Alsback H O	E	Winfield
Anderson F E	A	Clyde
Anglesmyer Jos	G	Winfield
Blake A E	H	Solomon City
Bratt Trumen	A	Corwin
Brown W H	B	Salina
Collier W M	D	Onaga
Davis John R	I	Winfield
Grant J H	F	Howard
Gray James	D	Schoharie
Griffith J S	I	Marion
Harter Henry	A	Marion
Hughes T E	C	Sedgwick
Hurd Melvin A	K	Fulton
Jennings J M lt	K	Wameg
Jennings B L	K	Louisville or Alma
Jones J A	D	Coffeyville
Kinsey Henry	A	Minneapolis
Knapp M H	H	Wier City
Kusley Noah	H	Valencia
Lewellen J L	F	Wellington
Makins Joseph	C	Onaga
McComb C C	E	Wellington
McCrum W c	D	Morehead
Mitchell John	G	Peabody
Moore G capt	K	Hiawatha
Moore W H	K	Hays City
Morrison W S lt	G	Sabetha
Moulton B 1st lt	G	Sabetha
Myers Levi c	E	Wellington
Myers Hiram	E	Wellington
Platt G W	I	Wichita
Popham E	A	Minneapolis
Rarick Jacob	A	Corbin
Reed J B s	C	Osage City
Shaw J W	B	Pliny
Sheldon S S	K	Reynolds Neb
Shriver Joshua	E	Towanda
Smith J W s	B	Athens
Snyder Henry	F	Thayer
Thompson J K	F	Ingalls
Walker G L	B	Augusta
Wright G J	D	Osborne
Wyland S	K	Fulton
Zimmerman D P	G	Kill Creek
Zimmerman John	G	Laura

SEVENTY-FIFTH INFANTRY THREE YEARS,

Colonels; J. J. Reynolds. J. U. Petit, M S. Robinson and Wm. O Brien.

Abney John wagoner	I	Oswego
Adamson J R	C	Fredonia
Barker Aaron c	F	Harper
Barker Rufus J s	I	Cawker City
Bartlett R A	G	Chetopa
Barton Wm R	E	Adel
Blossom E E	H	Brown's Grove
Boyd Jacob	C	Eldorado

Name		Co.	Residence
Brady John		A	Udall
Briggs Thomas	s	G	Neosho Rapids
Brooks N		I	Frankfort
Carr S H	lt	G	Chetopa
Chaney Nathan		H	Bronson
Denny Elias		C	Fredonia
DeWitt T L		H	Fawn Creek
DeWitt Clark		H	Opolis
Donley Samuel		K	Lincoln
Drake John H		A	Sedan
Earlywine Amos	m	H	Webster
Eubank David		E	Quenemo
Garberisk Geo	c	I	Topeka
Herron Daniel		B	Lane
Huzell H	s	A	Winfield
Jarrett J W	c	G	Burrton
Kennard E A		I	Elk City
Kinman N		H	Whiting
Knox		C	Burr Oak
Little J H		B	Jonesburg
Martin Geo		A	Perry
McKinney C G		A	Ottawa
Miller Jacob		K	Coffeyville
Myers Evan		A	Osawkee
Nixon Milton		A	Belle Plains
Pierson S W		H	Media
Rigley Daniel		C	Chetopa
Scott Winfield		D	Norway
Shadle R E		K	Green
Shick John		F	Lenora
Simmons E		I	Altoona
Smith J T	capt	G	Lincoln
Sperry J H	s	I	Thayer
Squires John	s	A	Miltonvale
Steffey H T		K	Clyde
Thompson J G		H	Mulvane
Tumbleson F M	h s		Louisburg
Underwood W R		F	Hutchinson
Wilcoxson E		K	Halstead
Wiley W T		B	Topeka

SEVENTY-SIXTH INDIANA INFANTRY — 30 DAYS' SERVICE.

Colonel, James Gavin

Name	Co.	Residence
Abbott A V	A	Humboldt
Avery W H	A	Spearville
Donelson E M	K	Cedarvale
Peck Wm	A	Burlington
Thomas J C	A	Iola
Tillson W S	E	Garnett
Whitlow W M	D	Topeka

SEVENTY-SEVENTH REGIMENT FOURTH CAVALRY, 3 YEARS.

Cols. Isaac P, Gray, L. J. Shuber, J. A. Platter, J. T. Deweese, H. P. Lamson.

Name		Co.	Residence
Anderson G W	s	C	Columbus
Barnard N W		E	Dennis
Beeson S M	s	H	Pawnee Valley
Bickham P D		L	Altamont
Brown C C		C	Circleville
Brown L T	s	C	Louisburg
Brown L J		D	Junction City
Brown W H		C	Western Park
Bryan W H		I	Sedan
Call S	c	D	Elgin
Cassidy Benj		L	Walnut
Connell W A	c	B	Wyandotte
Cortner J H		D	Lebo
Coulter Sam'l		G	Anthony

Name	Co.	Location
Cullison A	B	Independence
Davis J W	C	Blue Rapids
Deardoff E E	C	LaCynge
Dunlevy W H s	D	Eldorado
Eliot Morton	E	Peabody
Falconer M P	L	Lancaster
Ferguson J H	A	Sidney
Foley Timothy	B	Osborne
Foster S R	G	Anthony
Fradenburg J T	E	Eldorano
Gladden J W capt	G	State Center
Gore J W	H	Beloit
Guy A L	L	N Topeka
Hamilton H M	K	Baxter Springs
Henderson K M	K	Baxter Springs
Hendry J F	H	Keelville
Hicks J M		Elm Valley
Holliday D M	B	Harper
Horr W maj		Sterling
Hostetter J N	G	Mulvane
Howard John lt	F	Topeka
Howe John V	K	Beaumont
Hudson J	H	Hopewell
Hudson R L	L	Parsons
Hudson Willis	F	Phillipsburg
Jacobs Daniel	G	Burrton
Kirkham J C	K	Troy
Landers F T ·	F	Oneida
Leffler Ph	B	Lyndon
Lodge Henry lt	F	Erie
Lucky James	C	Cloverdale
Mall C F	M	Wamego
Marrs J S	I	Louisburg
Marshall Cy	D	Milan
McBride J F	F	Benton
Meek H H	A	Grenola or Rain Belt
Mershon John	I	Humboldt
Moore J O	G	Coffeyville
Moore Wm	D	Winfield
Murbarger Geo s	G	Topeka
Myers H C s	K	Baxter Springs
Manning Geo	H	Pleasanton
Platt Eli wagoner	C	Carbondale
Ragsdale Jasper	I	Topeka
Ramsey W	L	Benton
Robinett E	L	Ionia
Robinson Jas	F	Kiowa
Rogers S B	A	Olathe
Rowan Miles	E	Osborne
Sargent T J s	K	Garnett
Schmidt G W	M	Wyandotte
Shaw Jere	E	Dodge City
Simpson Edwin	A	Valley Center
Smith S	C	White Rock
Stackhouse Geo	C	Rossville
Stephenson W S	H	Hutchinson
Stone Alonzo s	F	Perry
Sullivan J P e	G	Logan
Summers E J	D	Hubbel Neb
Taggart A lt	D	Parsons
Thornton A J	H	Kansas City
Toliver J I	G	Lincoln
Toner Thos	C	Brookville
Townsend G	D	Westmoreland
Urie J Y capt	F	Carbondale
Van Note J L	E	Chetopa
Walton A J	E	Troy
Weaver W C	M	Radical
West Hugh q m s	B	Elk City
Wheeler Robert	F	Bridgeport
Williams J W	H	Redden
Williams W H s	I	Burlington

Lieut Col—Wm L. Farow.

Baird J R	C	Spearville
Fullwider Jacob	E	Carlyle
Hayes J W	A	Ft Scott
Heady R S c	A	Independence
John E	C	Burrton
Jones J	B	Little River
Pratt Alfred	B	Silver Lake
Ramsey A E	B	Freeman
Richter Elias	G	Purity

SEVENTY NINTH INFANTRY,—3 YEARS

Colonel—Frederic Kneffler.

Anderson John	C	Topeka
Boaz E C o s	C	Baldwin
Bardwell SW	C	Kingman
Boss Geo W c	H	Crown Point
Buhris C H	D	Madison
Caywood H V	K	Altoona
Carey Z M c	E	Lansing
Dangler T	C	Leon
Eastes J A	D	Andover
Eastes F M s	I	Great Bend
Ecret W E	E	Buffalo
Evans Geo I	K	Chetopa
Gibson Alfred	E	Erie
Hadley D W capt	K	Hutchinson
Hole H M	D	Chanute
Hollingsworth F	G	Elk Falls
Johntson J	E	Trego
Kline Joseph	C	Tecumseh
Lawhan L M	B	Hamilton
Lawson T S	A	Louisburg
Lewis W B 1st s	A	Neodesha
Little Azor	E	Durachen
Loucks Cornel us s	G	Crestline
Muth D M	B	Republic
Ray J W	K	Radical City
Sheets B C	B	Parsons
Short H N	E	Fredonia
Snavely David	H	Concordia
Southern C capt	F	Kansas City Mo
Thomas J A	D	Dodge City
Tully J	I	Independence
Warintz D	B	Baker
Watts Jacob	B	Padonia
White J H	C	McCune
Worthen I B	H	Melrose

EIGHTIETH INFANTRY, THREE YEARS.

Colonels, C Denby, Lewis Brooks, James L
Culbertson, Alfred Dale Owen

Alford W H	D	S dan
Bicknell Alfred c	C	Parsons
Bogener Wm	K	Coyville
Burch J S	E	Bulls City
Chennot T J	A	Clay Center
Clark Isaac	K	Corbin
Devin H J c	A	Mound City
Duncan John c	A	Mound City
Gilley John	D	Independence
Higgins Joseph	A	Atchison
Hill J P R	A	Toronto
Minor Jacob	I	Empire City
Moore W A	G	South Mound

Piper Conrad	C	Lerado, or Ruby
Queen Joseph S	B	Raceburg
Ragle N S	K	Yates Center
Ragle Alonzo s	K	Yates Center
Salley David	F	Fairview
Stephenson J A	H	Peabody
Stewart S T	A	White Church
Warren James A	E	Mendota
White Albert	D	Kirwin
Wilson Jesse	F	Freeman
Wolf J M lt	F	Winfield

EIGHTY-FIRST INFANTRY, THREE YEARS

Colonels, W. W. Caldwell, Horatio Woodbury, Ranna S. Moore, Oliver P. Anderson.

Bottorf Calvin	A	Carbondale
Clodel J T	G	Gaylord
Cole Thos. L adjt	I	Sedgewick City
Crandall C	C	Netherlands
Fry Geo T	R	Little River
Fulkinson Jasper	F.	Loretto
Green Daniel J	B	Welda
Hall Hendricks	E	Winfield
Hobbs Z H	D	Toronto
Houseworth J W c	B	Milan
Kramer Wm	D	Marmaton
May Reuben R	D	Turin
McAuley A M	F	Olivet
Midcap J S	B	Mankato
Miller R. C	C	Jordan Springs
Reed W T	G	Blue Rapids
Rosencrants W H	G	Cleardale
Shriwis Aug c	F	Buena Vista
Smith E F	I	Key
Smith W W	A	Dodge City
Starks A M	I	Downs
Sutton Z N	D	South Haven
Tayler Daniel c	K	Harlan
Timberlake W H adjt		Columbus
Tuttle L H capt	B	Baldwin
Wheetly Wm	G	Cedarvale
Worthington Wm	G	Densmore
Yack W F	C	Wichita
Zimmerman W H lt F		Olathe
Van Winkle J W lt H		Equity

EIGHTY SECOND INFANTRY, THREE YEARS.

Colonel, Morton C. Hunter.

Almond L C capt	E	Kingman
Barrick G C c	D	Garnett
Bearanger M 1st s	G	McCune
Bracken S c	H	Union Center
Briggs A C D c	C	Ft Scott or Iola
Campbell M M chaplain		N Topeka
Cantwell T J	C	N Topeka
Chase Aaron G capt	I	Millwood
Cummings W H	E	Clear Waters
Childs Philander	B	Paola
Duvall W R	H	McPherson
Fee Marcellus capt	F	Litchfield
Fullerton W B	F	Black Jack
Gaither Simon	F	Americus
Galbreath Ben tmst'r A		Westphalia
Galtry Albert s	B	Chanute
Grebe Geo W s	A	Center Ridge
Hemphill Wm s	C	Clay Center
Kelley Mathew ass't surg		Newton
Kennedy John	C	Clay Center

Name	Co.	Residence
Koont J G	F	August\
Lemon W H surgeon		Winchester
Lunday H E M lt	I	Humboldt
Markwell A	H	Anthony
Martindale A J	I	Bel··
McGrath Martin	F	Top·
Meek W R	B	Oxford
Miller R M	A	Beloit
Murphy Wm .	D	Roland
Reeve H C	I	Topeka
Rich W R	B	Nickerson
Robbins Geo	B	Clyde
Robison T J	F	Quincy
Robison J F	F	Washington
Roseberry C W	C	Arkansas City
Saunders J A	F	Elk City
Saudners H	H	Toronto
Story D S capt	H	Durachen
Study Isaac	C	Cedarvale
Swearengen J W	F	Garnett
Irick Jacob	D	Brownsville
Weeks Joseph s	E	Americus
Wise John H	G	Mayfield

EIGHTY-THIRD INFANTRY, THREE YEARS.

Colonels, Benj. J. Spooner, Geo. H. Scott

Name	Co.	Residence
Babcock C C s	A	Hollenburg
Bailey S J c	C	Independence
Beach D C hosp std	I	Winfield
Blaisdel T A	H	Birrton
Brum Jacob	D	Junction City
Chisman W	I	Augusta
Cloud Daniel	C	Osborn
Crandall D K	C	Menoken
Ewbanks G W	H	Marion
Feighan J W lt	K	Emporia
Hess David	F	Ft Scott
Houze Michael	C	Wyadotte
Horton G L.	A	Harvevsville
Hunt J B	B	Eureka
Isgrigg S B	A	Walnut
Leynas Enoch	H	Walnut
McNair A L	A	Manhattan
Mercer Wm 1st lt	H	Washington
Morris Geo W capt	G	La Monts Hill
Renner Ignatius c	G	Andover
Richardson M A s	A	Leanna
Schmidt John	E	Peters
Shepard J L	B	Hutchinosn
Sisson Z B	K	Garnett
Thompson J A	A	Peabody
Stoneking Martin	A	Garnett

EIGHTY-FOURTH INFANTRY, THREE YEARS.

Cols. Nelson Trusler, A. J. Neff, Martin B. Miller.

Name	Co.	Residence
Addington W S c	A	Eldorado
Arment A B s	I	Winheld
Ball John C	I	Burlington
Burket Dan	B	Ashland or Holton
Cochren N J	B	Sterling
Craw R B	K	Peabody
Cook W J	I	Frankfort
Crowder H D	G	Chanute
Davis H	C	Lone Oak
Eaton Peter	G	Spearville
Frazier J D	E	Independence
Green J H	B	Washington
Green T H	B	Washington

Hall Izri	G	Chanute
Harvey W	G	Eldorado
Hiatt W F s	H	Hiattville
Holler Fred	G	Topeka
Holloway A 1	I	Wichita
Jewell W D	I	Hutchinson
Kelsey S H	I	Atchison
Kilmer Thos	H	Topsy
Keenan Oscar	B	Lyndon
Kerr M A m		Flood
Kirby Henry surgeon		Osage City
Kirkwood A W s	B	Marysville
Little David	K	Ellinwood
Little James H c	I	Salem
Mahony Clem	E	Sterling
Mendenhall C S s	I	Osage City
Morgan M	E	Dundee
Murray Ed	E	Marvin
Neff Arch	K	Lyndon
Pendergrass E	A	Achilles
Potter A P	I	Coffeyville
Shidler Ed	K	Dragoon
Silvey W T e	G	Cawker City
Somers Chas	I	Republic
Stephenson Esla	D	Pratt
Temple Geo	F	Cecil
Taylor R W	D	Wamego
Thompson L	B	Netawaka
Wesley Geo	A	Solomon
Wilkinson R A	F	Waytown
Wilson Amos L s	K	Lyndon
Wilson L T m	K	Lyndon
Woodbury N	H	Washington

EIGHTY FIFTH INFANTRY, THREE YEARS SERVICE.

Colonels, John P Baird, Alex B Crane,

Bacus J W s	A	Howard
Baker Samuel	C	Iola or Lansing
Barrett John s	D	Mentor
Benight H J s	E	Humboldt
Benjamin W J c	K	Burlington
Bowsher J B	A	Bull City
Bussinger M C	K	Reno Center
Carney W H	I	Strawn
Cochran C D	H	Fellsburg
Colwell Geo	A	Rosehall
Cooprider J s	K	Kinga a
Clark Reuben s	F	Naomi
Dart L T		Colony
Eckard M A	I	Wetmore
Engle J H	B	Burlingame
Finney D W 1st s	A	Neo Falls
Fortner John c	E	Hale
Furnas D s	I	Wichita
Graham D E	A	Independence
Grimes R R s	C	Severy
Gurley J A lt	A.	Le Roy
Heath Jacob	A	Neodesha Falls
Henderson M lt	E	Elk Falls
Higby Lewis	D	Barnesville
Holmes G W	K	Wichita
Hoover Isaac	D	Coyville
Huffman Ira A	A	Anthony
Johnson D W	F	Waubaunsee
Jones W L	E	South Mound
Joslin Raymond	E	Caldwell
Maples Silas	C	Trenton
McDonald P H	H	Ashland
McKee John s	J	Grenola
Mitchell D s	D	Weir City

Name	Co.	Residence
Nash Caleb c	I	Cedarvale
Peterson R J	G	Centerville
Powell A J	K	N Lawrence
Pritchard C R	E	Cherryvale
Reaser Daniel	F	Hallowell
Redman J H	D	Sidney
Reeder Wm capt	D	Troy
Shoemaker P A	E	Guelph
Shuler S	K	N Topeka
Smith W J	E	Ottawa
Terril C A	E	Parsons
Thompson Wm	F	Corning
Troutman J F c	E	Colony
Tucket D	A	Independence
Voils W H	H	Wellington
Wellman L C	D	Climax
Youmans J E	D	Wellington

EIGHTY-SIXTH INFANTRY, THREE YEARS' SERVICE.

Cols—Orville S. Hamilton, Geo F. Dick

Name	Co.	Residence
Alexander J R c	D	Richland
Baker W T	H	Girard
Baldis John	D	Rural or Williamstown
Black John D	F	Ashton
Briggs J C	E	Dodge City
Burk G W	K	Rossville
Bush John s	I	Galena
Calton W T	D	Matfield Green
Caldwell J N	E	Parsons
Cowdery L G lt	G	Osage City
Cowdry J A	G	N Topeka
Collins Geo M	G	Beloit
Conner C P	C	Paola
Crane A J	C	Chautauqua
Davis Morgan	F	Harper
Dimmick D J	D	Dresden
Forbes W J	K	McPherson
Gould James	D	Anthony
Harmon R J	A	Cover
Harris Alex	K	Oswego
Henton J O s	I	Junction City
Hickson J W s	F	Bronson
Higgins G H	A	Jonesburg
Hoddy C R c	E	Morantown
Howard Tighlman A 1st s	K	Ottawa
Kelley E	A	Independence
Kempton Dan'l chaplain		Burden
Kiser Alex	K	Louisburg
Kiser W W	E	Louisburg
Lukens Joseph	I	Walnut
Lytle Edward	I	Salem
Maltbie Joshua c	G	Sallee
Mathesley W J	E	Nickerson
McCormick J I	A	Topeka
McNett Newton	E	Maple Hill
Michels John s	I	Greenwich
Moore Jacob S	A	Liberty
Morrison W H	E	Alma
Mosier Harwey	D	Mulvane
Odell Thos A capt	C	Rural (Dec'd)
Odell Alfred s	C	Dexter
Owings Ephram	E	LaCygne
Orr M E	H	Pratt
Patton Geo	I	Valencia
Peed Henry	K	Central City
Reynolds M	C	Garnet
Rowe J D	H	Monmouth
Schoolcraft John	C	Wamego

Sigler W H H s	D	Floral
Slane Lane	I	Arlington
Snyder J W s	G	Sedgwick
Spillman R B capt	K	Manhattan
Starry N H	E	Louisbu g
Stephens R N s	D	Burdeu
Stevens Lewis capt	D	Floral
Stearn L M	B	Ft Scott
Stoops R W	A	Sulphur Springs
Swank Wilson	K	Osborne
Swartz Eli musician	C	Wyandotte
Sylvester C O 1st lt	C	Olathe
Trout A J	A	Herman
Warrick G C	C	Brush Creek
Williams J T	G	Elk Falls
Wils n J W	H	Mulberry Grove
Wolford H	B	Howard
White John	B	Wellington

EIGHTY-SEVENTH INFANTRY, THREE YEARS TERM.

Cols. Kline G. Shryock, Newell Gleason.

Adamson Isaiah	D	Osage Mission
Babcock Robert	A	Chanute
Ball Daniel N	D	Grantville
Ball A M	D	Caldwell
Barnett W S c	E	Udall
Berget Philip	G	White Rock
Birch Andrew	B	Delphi
Bousman G W	H	Stafford
Bower Wm c	G	Ness City
Bowman J W s	H	Prairie View
Brown Daniel L	H	Concordia
Burch L	D	Mona
Carter John N	E	Peoria
Davis James H	G	Arkansas City
Evans Geo H	B	Topeka
Fierce Henry c	H	Rush Center
Finch E S	H	Robinson
Fires David	H	Blue Rapids
Fouts Jacob D s	A	St. John
Grow Wm	G	Columbus
Hatter Andrew s	D	Baltimore
Heikman L H	F	Elk Chase Co
Hight Geo W	B	Empire City
Hough C R	A	Pleasanton
Jones S	E	Robinson
Kilmer J M	E	Rosedale
Martin A A c	H N Topeka or Augusta
Matsol Jacob	I	Naomi
McDonald E	G	Coffeyville
Nichols Solomon	A	Carbondale
Nowles Geo	A	Elk Falls
Payne F s	A	Kingman
Poston Henry	A	Netawaka
Poston Sam V	A	Netawaka
Post J M	A	Magnolia
Quinn Robt	K	Toronto
Reader Daniel	B	Cheney
Robbins Redin	C	Ottawa
Robbins Wm S	C	Grafton
Robinson J H	I	Washington
Roof J M	G	North Topeka
Ross H S	E	Brush Creek
Sayers T J	A	Roy
Sell John B		Republic
Short Edward	F	Clifton
Smith J R	E	Caldwell
Smith Orlen	E	Ft Scott
Soper W F	E	Neodesha
Spurry S W	I	Cherokee

Steel J M	A	North Topeka
Steel Sam H	H	Burlington
Stotler Harrison	F	Bronson
Troutman J T c	E	Beloit
Vandever J H 1st lt	E	Newton
Wapler Otto	A	Beloit
Westheffer Elias	H	Eudora
Willey W H	A	Parsons
Woonsley John	A	Alexander

EIGHTY-EIGHTH INFANTRY, THREE YEARS
TERM.

Colonels, Geo Humphrey, Cyrus E. Briant.

Awald Jacob	D	Clyde
Burrell Anderson	K	Altoona
Boggs Martin	F	Douglass
Campbell Lewis	G	Vining
Cotrill J L	A	Stafford
Criss M W s	I	Topeka
Culver E C	B	Elk City
Delano Geo	H	ecttsville
Delano J C	H	ledgwood
Farmer A c	E	Anthony
Henning John s	E	La Cygne
Henry S C	H	La Cygne
Harshberger DW capt		Vinland
Huff T G		Saronberg
Hull J T	C	Ionia
Irwin Geo A chaplain		Council Grove
King Peter	F	Pipe Creek
Klingaman John	I	Marysville
Kreigh Geo s	F	Grainfield
Lidy Daniel	A	Chepstow
McClelland H C	E	Altamont
Middleton John c	I	Blaine
Mil'er Z ch m	D	Iola
Miller L P	K	Emporia
Mills T C	A	Carlton
Mooney O	C	Towanda
Nohlstine J H s	C	Geuda Springs
Notstine Isiah	D	Browns Grove
Pfaff Geo	B	Oswego
Randall A J c	K	Eldorado
Raefsyder John	L	Pipe Creek
Rhodes Isaac	D	Colorado
Ricle H H	K	Chetopa
Robert Amos	F	Sedan
Sipe Seth M	E	Ibaton
Snider Alfred	D	Miltonvale
Stoner C C	B	Nelson
Walters D s	F	Chalk Mound
Walker F G	I	St George
Ward H	C	Morehead
Washburn E	K	N Topeka
Waterline J A s	C	Geuda Springs
Whitaker C A c	C	Cawker City
Young Hiram 1st s	B	Nelson

EIGHTY-NINTH INFANTRY, THREE YEARS
TERM.

Col. Charles D. Murray.

Arbaugh Perry s	E	Independence
Baldwin L E	C	Washington
Bartley Joseph	C	Empire City
Barr Stephen	E	Pittsburg
Boerstler M	I	Chanute
Bradbury W A	C	Lyle
Burns Wm capt	F	Vermilion
Burkhead N H s	H	Beloit.

Burnton D	K	Moline
Burr J H	A	Waverly
Biddle Henry s	A	Pawnee Station
Clingenpal Wm m		Peotone
Cook Peter M	E	Everett
Crabbs J M q m		Hutchinson
Davis Nathan	C	Moline
Dorley J H	G	Doster
Dillon Wm capt	K	Lawrence
Farley P H s	D	Lincoln
Fifer Sam	F	Burr Oak
Foucher H W	D	Lyndon
Preed Noah	D	Neodesha
Goul J W	B	Cherokee
Goul Christian	A	Monmouth
Griffis David	C	Toledo
Hall Joseph L 1st s	E	Concordia
Haller Jacob	H	Wetmore
Harman Wm	D	Pittsburg
Harman J R c	D	Baxter Spring
Harvey C W s	C	Quakervale
Hull E G		Cherryvale
Helm Geo	I	Fall River
Hull E G	A	Elk Falls
Jackson Joseph	E	Cawker City
Jackson J W s	E	Downs
Johnson Z M lt	A	Wichita
Kates Richard	C	Michigan Valley
Kanfman Jacob c	A	Jonesburg
Lewis Chester	E	Norway
Loofborrow J N	E	Scandia
Long Addison	D	Louisburg
Markland G capt	D	Warrensburg Mo
Martz Smith	H	Council Grove
McClure Henry	I	South Cedar
McHugh H B	K	Yates Center
Mickel Philip s	F	Cherryvale
Miller J Y	E	·Mankato
Miller J C	H	North Topeka
O'Harra Chas T s	E	Concordia
Oran Albert	A	Palmer
Powers H C	E	Independence
Ratcliff John C	D	Pittsburg
Reynolds D P c	K	Colorado
Ross W B	G	Hope
Sims Elijah	G	Preston
Silings F M c	A	Kingman
Smith Ichabod 1st s	C	Mona
Stanley J B	E	Trivoli
Taylor Joseph c	D	Lyons
Thomas A J	D	Burden
Way P P	E	Talmo or Seapo
Wells Wm	A	Malta
Warner J W	A	Paola
Wilson J C	E	Prairie View
Winslow J C c	C	Tonganoxie
Wood B F	K	Winfield
Woolen J H	F	Burr Oak
Wonsler John	A	Alexander
Younkin S	G	Garfield

NINTIETH REGIMENT FIFTH CAVALRY
THREE YEARS.

Colonels—R R Stewart, Felix W Graham,
Thomas H Butter.

Anderson James	K	Newton
Bellville Lander	G	Tipton
Bellville David	G	Tipton
Bleam D C	D	Osborne
Brown Hugh A c	A	Fulton
Bush D W	A	Walnut

Name	Co.	Place
Champion F M o s	A	Catlin
Campbell Geo H	B	Culver
Coke Henry vet surg	H	South Center
Denny S P	E	Winchest r
Douglas James H c	E	Cyrus
Dunbar D T	H	Wichita
Duncan D D	M	Belmont
Elliott A O	E	Torrance
Fairchilds J H	I	Independence
Fisher R H	A	Kennekuck
George Dempsey	A	Erie
Gorham J A c	F	Winchester
Graham C H s	F	Surich
Greer J E lt	F	Grass
Groat Richard	B	Emerald
Harlan Joshua	I	Belleville
Harman A J	A	Carbondale
Hillman W R,	C	Sedan
Huselton H F	A	Somerset
Heath T R	L	Lane
Johnson A	F	Brooks
Jones T N c	L	Brush Creek
Kingdon S D	H	Eskridge
Lockwood W.	E	Wall Street
Lockmiller J	I	Elk Falls
Mahan M T	K	Grenola
Martin J S	H	Dodge City
McClarg A B	M	El Dorado
McCullough J A lt	L	Pratt
McCullough H B	H	Hartford
Masterman B F hosp st'd		Independence
McGlanahan Gus	D	Leavenworth
Massoth Henry	D	Piqua
Meek M M	G	Grenola
lewhinney B F	H	Melvern
Murray A G lt	G	Marysville
Miller A L s	K	Junction City
Miller C W s		Florence
Moss Jacob E	L	Vidette
New John B	A	Ford
Nichols A W	I	Longton
Overly Wm	D	Winfield
Perkins Elisha	E	Columbus
Pilkerton W H lt	G	Wa Keeny
Pillington W M	L	Atchison
Poor John T s	F	Grass
Pope F M s	G	Dodge City
Proctor Discor	I	Atchison
Ritter Henry	E	Kirwin
Robins Enoch	A	Bulls City
Rock Samuel	E	New Basil
Routh J T B	B	Garnett
Raszell Geo H	H	Wayne
Sampson J O	I	Haynesville
Scott Louis	L	Waco
Shaver Jacob	G	Bashan
Shroyer Samuel	I	Marysville
Smiley Thos H	H	Andover
Spidle David	C	Circleville
Stober Urias W c	B	Clifton
Stalker Henry artificer E		South Cedar
Street J W	I	Fall River
Sweet A Y	I	Oswego
Thackrey Sam'l	H	Manhattan
Topp E M c	F	Maud
Wallace John H	I	WaKeeny
Ware Isaac C	A	Gr enleaf
Webb John P c	C	M nroe
William C S s	I	Longton
Wise F C	H	Douglas

NINETY FIRST INFANTRY, THREE YEARS— EXCEPT COMPANIES H, I, AND K, SIX MONTHS AND ONE YEAR.

Colonel, John Mehringer.

Bowers L H	H	(1 yr) Harper
Calvin J W	D	Floral
Denny G Cs	A	Burlingame
Dutton Milton U	F	Galeua
Essex James	H	(1 yr) Harrison
Gadberry John P	C	Bronson
Gay John D s	F	Yates Center
Helmick A C	A	Independence
Henderson J J	H	(6m) Mission Creek
Johnson J T	C	Peru
Lamar S U	E	Williamsburg
Marshall Wm	D	Lincoln
Miller W M c	C	Wilmot
Mullin John	H	(1 yr) Chester, Neb
Monday W	I	Broms
Mosier Sol	I	(1 yr) Blaine
Mullenour F R	K	Chetopa
Oliver J W c	F	Wellington
Peek Ira H	B	Galena
Robertson L L	B	Mound Valley
Rooney John	K	(6 mos) Phillipsburg
Shroyer James	K	(6 mos) Blue Rapids
Simpson W F	D	Arkansas City
Smith W H H	I	(1 yr) Beaumont
Wilson Lemuel	C	Polo
Woods Geo	I	Concordia

NINETY SECOND REGIMENT—Organization not completed—four companies recruited for it were joined to the Ninty-Third Rgm t.

NINETY THIRD INFANTRY, THREE YEARS TERM.

Colonels, De Witt C. Thomas.

B m'ks T J	D	Matfield Green
Bartlets S J capt	F	Baxter Springs
Elkins James	C	Somerset
Eick Peter	B	Otto
Foster E P lt	E	Liberty
Fuller Wm	E	White Rock
Fuller J W	F	Prospect
Fullen J W	F	Scandia
Hacker A B c	E	Parsons
Pearce Wm C	D	Everest
Ridinger D lt	A	Newton
Stringer Eli lt	A	Edgerton
Tannehill W D lt	E	Argonia
Trent J E	A	Independence
Tull W H	B	Wichita
Welch C lt	E	Parsons
Wells F M	D	Wellington

NINETY FOURTH REGIMENT—Not Organized

NINETY-FIFTH REGIMENT—Not Organized

NINETY-SIXTH REGIMENT—Not Organized

NINETY-SEVENTH INFANTRY — THREE YEARS SERVICE.

Colonels—Robt F Catterson: Adam G Cavens

Anderson Lewis	A	Erie
Anderson Calvin	B	Uniontown
Burcham A J	C	Fulton

Bough Thomas	A	Cedarville
Busby D W o	D	Clyde
Butcher W T capt	E	Fredonia
Cheatwood J	B	DeSoto
Clever John	C	Cato
Climer A s	E	Beaumont
Coffman A J s	B	Sedgewick City
Corwin J E lt	A	Sabetha
Courtney Prentiss	B	Rockville
Davis S	D	Council Grove
Demer S M	K	Augusta
Detro James	D	Westmoreland
Drake S	B	Piedmont
Draper S H	B	Augusta
Duling C C	F	Long Island
Eek Peter	H	Independence
Forsyth A P lt	I	Liberty
Hocker Wm	D	Chalk Mound (dead)
Hapenny A C	B	Lamar
Hubbel Henry E	F	Howard
Johnson W H q m		Topeka
Johnson John H	A	Woodlawn
Kaufman Nich	I	Melvern
Kitch J M	H	Columbus
Light George	F	Ida or Hubbel
Long Edward c	E	Humboldt
Madden John	B	Cottonwood Falls
Nihart J W	H	Arcadia
Nied Jacob		Industry
Nees David		Independence
Nelson J M	B	Independence
Payne M	I	Garnett
Phillips S J s	H	Junction City
Randolph L A M	K	Fontana
Reed R M c	F	Pratt
Reynolds A	A	Lapland or Easton
Reynolds Simeon	I	White Cloud
Rodgers T U s	D	Parkersville
Rodgers Howard	D	Westmoreland
Shadley F	G	Fulton
Shultz Emanuel	H	Brush Creek
Stone J E	E	Union Center
Thompson Salathiel s	A	Fairview
Wadsock Ernest	H	Douglas

NINETY-EIGHTH REGIMENT—Not organized

NINETY-NINTH REGIMENT INFANTRY,
THREE YEARS TERM.

Cols. Alex. Fowler, Josiah Farrar.

Andis R P capt	B	Girard
Baldwin Jonathan	B	Eldorado
Barker James	D	Otto Cowley Co
Bartholomew Chas	E	Mt Liberty
Baldwin Joseph	B	Salmon City
Bray A Matthias s	G	Montana
Bray James	G	Montana
Budd Elliott	H	Burlington
Drennen Benj	A	Iola or Baldwin
Dutton James	A	Grenola
Enfield John	E	Mapleton
Enyart Thos	I	Kirwin
Eply Josiah T s	D	Kingman
Farrar Josiah capt	D	Empire City
Fowler Alex col		Uniontown
Gaskell Adam J	H	Lawrence
Gibbs A M	B	Ft Scott
Griffey Geo W	D	Chapman
Gilbert Moses c	K	Thayer
Hale John A	A	Grenola
Hamlin J M lt	D	Ft Scott

Harvey John lt	D	Grenola
Hauscheldt Jacob	E	Eskridge
Holly J D	G	Chanute
Jones W A	K	Hillsdale
Karnes S D c	E	Hubbel Neb
Kendall J P	G	Hesper
Kramer H S	E	Clyde
Lindeman C H s	K	Our Carter
Loux Charles L o-s	C	Westmoreland
Louther Arnold	E	Columbus
Long J F	I	New Lancaster
Mackey Wm lt	C	Pleasanton
Marley Orran	G	Princeton
Maxson Wm	F	Roxbury
McGonigal J B lt	I	Solomon
Meeks A S	I	Arnold
Mearill Geo W s	A	Moline
Milnor Amos	B	Madison
Oliver David	C	Downs
Rarden Wm	F	Piedmont
Rogers Thomas	G	Prairie Center
Saylor John	K	Douglas
Shafer Joseph	E	Hutchinson
Shaw John	K	St George
Shidler C L s	E	Leon
Shipman J J	B	Burr Oak
Shaw M F	F	Jonesburg
Slifer Levi	B	Medicine Lodge
Smith Edward C	B	Centralia
Smith Geo W o s	E	Clyde
Thornton T L	E	Fredonia
Tillotson F	A	Moline
Tyner H C	B	Axtell
Whitehurst V	B	Beloit
Williams A	A	Altamont
Wilson W M	A	Madison
Walker G F lt	F	Cabin Creek I T

ONE HUNDREDTH   INFANTRY,   THRREE
YEARS TERM.

Colonels, Chas Case, Sanford J Stoughton,
Albert Heath, Ruel M Johnson.

Atwater M L	C	Neuchatel
Bodine D C s	A	Neodesha
Burnside Wm lt	G	Ft Scott
Cleland James	F	Halstead
Falk John W	F	Valley Falls
Fullerton James	F	Thayer or Morehead
Fritlenger Geo	H	Scandia
Frisct H C	A	Osborne
Grubb Allen	E	Wellington
Hall John M	A	Raymond
H mm Christopher	D	Newton
Haswell L R	K	Kimeo
Haynes Frank	K	Cedarville
Hilton L L s	B	Arkansas City
Hooper James	E	Armistead
Ingraham L D	C	Lyons
Jarvis Cements	B	Ova
Jones J B	H	Mt Ida
Kine J C	D	Monitor
Lucas G W	I	Elk City
Miller Alonzo	D	Peabody
r S R	C	Nickerson
e D J s	H	Sedan
Olinger Cyrus	A	Mt Ida
Pierce Geo M	A	Larned
Porter E A	H	Newton
Rathbun G lt	H	Raymond
Rovell W W	D	Carmi

Name		Co.	Place
Sherlock Eli J capt		A	Wyandotte
Sewell I G		G	Bulls City
Sperlock C C		A	Roxbury
Stansfield R T		K	Republic
Suppenaugh I		B	Ova
Timmons D c		G	Mound Valley
Timmons Wm		G	Mound Valley
Trump Wm H		D	Raymond
Waterbury J J		I	Clyde

ONE HUNDRED AND FIRST INFANTRY, THREE YEARS TERM.

Cols Wm. Garver, Thomas Doan.

Name		Co.	Place
Andrews Geo W	c	E	Burlington
Bacar James G		A	Topeka
Banister J N	lt	D	Pleasanton
Bennett O R		B	Elk Falls
Bennett J W			Elk Falls
Bever Elijah		A	Neosho Falls
Biggs M M		B	Sedgewick City
Campbell J M	s	B	Sedgewick City
Carson J M		A	Lyndon
Cook Wm O		E	Emporia
Culbertson D F	lt	H	Dragoon
Davis Daniel	c	D	Burr Oak
Folland Elias		D	Almena
Folland Joseph		D	Almena
Franks D O		A	Mulvane
Franks B F		A	Mulvane
Green Oscar		F	Lyndon
Gunning Sinclair		I	Mound Valley
Henley J R		I	Lebo
Hoddy A P		D	Belleville
Hudley A		D	Cherryvale
Johnson Job		A	Clements
Johnson W P	m	B	Cora
Logan James		K	Corning
Loer T B	capt	H	Belle Plaine
McCormick M E		D	Hymer
Miller Adam A		B	Coffeyville
Miller Geo W		K	Jewell City
Piersol Silas		D	Ottawa
Ratcliff Thos A		C	Columbus
Reveal M M		A	Council Grove
Roil John		D	Hartford
Royal J E		D	Burr Oak
Shaw J S	c	F	Minneapolis
Silver John		G	Farlington
Sims N B		K	Kingman
Small Reuben O		I	Sterling
Smith Samuel		D	Madison
Smyers D P		K	Laura
Snethen G E		E	Oakwood
Stanbrough J B		D	Brooks
Swann D L		H	Mound Valley
Taylor J T	s	E	Chase
Tyner B W		K	Kingman
Wheeler S J		D	Edna
Whicker J A	s	A	Almena
Whitright J		G	Canton
Wilson J R	s	F	Fordham
Winebrenner j		G	Dorrance
Wonderly I	s		Independence
Wright G H		H	Yates Center
Wherrett J N	adj		Vestsburg

MORGAN RAID REGIMENTS—Minute men—
Consisted of a bevy 12 regiments,
No. 102 to 114 inclusive.

Clayton Thos	D 1 2	Sedan
Davis L C	K 102	Coffeyville
Davis John capt	K 1 2	Coffeyville
Broe Nelson	F 104	Nelson
King J D capt	1 4	Wyandotte
Simmons Wm	C 104	Rantoul
Bever Henry	E 1 5	Concordia
Sloan J D	A 105	Roy
Persell W D	G 1 6	Leota, Neb
Beaman F c	C 1 7	Douglass
Jones J J	C 1 8	Burlington
Smith J H	D 108	Fredonia
Cornwell S	K 110	Galva
Gates John	H 110	Iola
Nuss S E	110	Ward
Bowman J	D 111	Alma
Schrick G	C 112	Cherryvale
De Voe R R	H 113	Lerado
O'Donald B	B 114	Dodge City
Hungate A J capt	1 4	Topeka

ONE HUNDRED AND FIFTEENTH INFANTRY,
SIX MONTHS' REGIMENT.

Colonel, John R Mahan.

Ball Wm E s	B	Newton
Bent J J capt	I	Topeka
Beauchamp Geo capt	K	Maud
Biddle A J lt	I	Silver Lake
Bland Enoch F	A	Beloit
Bland J O D c	A	Concordia
Boret J J	I	Burlingame
urnside J H	B	Chetopa
Chance H L	D	Sutphens Mill
Dunlavy John s	D	Junction City
Edminson F	C	Mapleton
Funkhouser B F	K	Eskridge
Goff D W s	E	Emporia
Gwinn J F lt	G	Topeka
Hammond Wm F	E	Altamont
Hill Henry T	H	Welda
Hill Henry	F	Girard
Hobbs Joshua	E	Neuchatel
Ingle N T	E	Hoyt
Johnson C M 1st s	K	Wamego
King G W	I	Xenia
King Geo W	I	Baldwin
Kephart Wm	B	La Cygne
Larew Joseph	B	Burlington
Manning J	E	Beaumont
McClure G W	B	Irving
McDaniel G W	B	Le Roy
McCutchan W F	B	Richmond
Myers J G	H	Byron
Myrs J S	A	Irving
Naylor David	E	Topeka
Owen W H H	A	West Asher
Patton J T	F	Cleveland
Popham J M	K	Ottumwa
Rector James	K	Mt Pleasant
R el Amos	F	Girard
Scott John F	I	South Cedar
Watson J H	E	Altoon
West Geo	E	Sever
Wilsey J L s	D	Kingman
Wilson J A	G	Pleasanton
Wiley J R		Sedgwick

SIX MONTHS REGIMENT.

Col. Wm. C. Kise.

Name	Co.	Residence
Bennitt J L c	B	Mankato
Bingamon Joseph	F	Pomona
Boyd W W	B	Cherryvale
Brannon T H	C	Rossville
Cneney H A c	I	Cuba
Clark Mitchel B	C	Haskell
Cogswell J P	F	Carbondale
Connell W A c	I	Wyandotte
Cory A L	A	Hadley
Davison N s	K	Douglas
Dollarhide Ira F	B	Greensburg
Ferguson Robert s	C	Galesburg
Fernald Ch H	I	Topeka
Fleming M K	B	Ottawa
Forbes L A	K	Farms
Forbes Jacob	H	Hampton
Flessia Christian		Gypsum Creek
Green W H s	A	Glen Elder
Gilfillan D G	D	Independence
Glick Nathan	I	Beattie
Gregory Alex	D	Independence
Guest T H	H	Grafton
Harrison T J c	D	Auburn
Haner H H		Olathe
Hexton Jonah	H	Ellsworth
Henry Charles	C	Mound City
Holliday W C lt	C	Harveysville
Hutton Wm	C	Argonia
Macklin J E capt	K	Ft Leavenworth
Mahoney W H	H	Blue Mound
Matthews P B	E	Salina
Morrison James	B	London
Morrow J H	D	Oskaloosa
Near J G	B	Augusta
Newman Geo W	C	Matanzas
Olinger J C	K	Plum Grove
Perrine R M	D	Cawker City
Pine Sam'l s	I	Cherryvale
Purcells J W	B	Lawrence
Poinsette W B s	D	Quenemo
Rankin B S	D	Kingston
Sheals John	H	Centropolis
Shidler Isaac	H	Allegan
Shipps C T	C	St George
Shoemaker J B	C	Haskell
Smith Benj	A	Neosho Falls
Stafford W H s	C	Clear Water
Swartz Cyrus	D	Minneapolis
Whistler J H	E	Eldorado
Tyler H C	H	Neosho Falls

ONE–HUNDRED AND SEVENTEENTH IN-
FANTRY, SIX MONTHS' REGIMENT.

Colonel, Thomas J Brady.

Name	Co.	Residence
Baker Wm H	G	Independence
Ba'linger John c	B	Havan
Barnhill A J	I	Fredoni
Baxter S W s	G	Olesburg
Beal A A c	I	Wellington
Brewer W F	G	Yates Center
Brown A	G	Kingman
DeMoss Wm A	B	Larne t
Edwards Wm	C	King-ton
Ellot Emery A	H	Belle Plaine
Falkner Andrew	G	Dodge City
Faris D S	I	Winchester
Gabbart H C s	I	Augusta

Name	Co.	Town
Green Elias S	D	Chanute
Houston W J	I	Tabor
Irby S W s	F	Independence
Kendall H s	B	Ft Scott
Kintl A A	B	Phillipsburg
Logan David	I	Winchester
Martin W H H	G	Belle Plaine
Mathers B F	I	Benton
McKenney P s	G	Girard
McLin J H	K	Union Center
Montgomery N C	D	Burlington
Morris L M	G	Scandia
Orem W	F	Great Bend
Roberts J L s	D	Morantown
Rushton Joshua	A	Red Cloud
Solomon S	C	Centropolis
Stolker E L 1st s	G	Hoyt
Tout John	B	Thayer
Walters W T	G	Emporia
Weaver C c	F	Everest
Weyman S D	G	Jordan Springs
Zeigler Wm M	C	Hays City

ONE-HUNDRED AND EIGHTEENTH IN-
FANTRY, SIX MONTHS' REGIMENT.

Colonel, Geo. W Jackson.

Name	Co.	Town
Abbott F M	K	Urbana
Becker John T c s		Glen Elder
Blue David A	A	Norton
Burton Wm	A	Auburn
Cable C H	B	Yoxall
Deardorf T C	G	Minneapolis
Friedline M H	B	Fredonia
Gallion P H	D	Grenola
Good Jacob	B	Loretta
Glemmer Peter c	B	Waterloo
Graves C W	G	Topeka
Holloway O J c	H	Lawrence
Hunter E W s		Kingman
Jackson Wm	I	Madison
Kilgore William	K	Scottsville
Klingerman Wm.	A	Lincoln
Lopshire Joseph	I	Lincoln
McKinney Jas s	G	Newton
Micher M c	B	Baxter Springs
Miller Solomon	K	Caldwell
Moulder F C c	H	Hutchinson
Porter J C lt	B	Sterling
Pugh J L	I	Thompsonville
Reynolds John	K	White Rock
Shackelford J W	K	Corning
Sinclair A	G	Cloverdale
Smith W H	E	Osage Mission
Stalnacher W H c	K	Kansas City, Mo
Steinberger Ira lt	K	Erie
Underwood W W s	C	Dexter
Warrensburg J W	K	Centralia
Wells C A	G	Heber
West Minns	K	Leon
Wheeler J O	C	Blue Rapids
Wilson W L	F	Coloma
Wood M C s	H	Goddard

ONE HUNDRED AND NINTEENTH REGIMENT,
SEVENTH CAVALRY, THREE YEARS.

Cols. J. P. C. Shanks, Thomas M. Browne.

Name	Co.	Town
Authon Fred	F	LaCygne
Baker B	E	Hutchinson
Bales B F capt	I	Cawker City

Name	Co.	Place
Bradford J M	C	Galena
Coates Daniel	B	Burlington
Cummings James	F	Pleasant Run
Dorsey Charles G	L	Galena
Drake R W c	M	Harper
Dukate J S	F	Independence
Dumont John F lt	D	Topeka
Eubanks Geo S	C and F	Argonia
Ewtan R R	D	Cottonwood Falls
Fairchild H c	A	Fredonia
Galconer D	B	Lancaster
Ferguson Frank c	C	Ellsworth
Fleming M K	L	Ottawa or Atchison
Frazier W W s	F	Westmoreland
Freeman R C c	B	Mulberry Grove
Gardner J J	A	Arcadia
Hand J M	C	Lawrence
Hardesty A	C	Lincoln
Harding Ben J	F	Leavenworth
Haskins N	A	Fall River
Henderson S B s	L	Scio
Hinos F M	C	Atchison
Huffman S D	D	Sedan
Hunt T S	D	Chanute
Jarritt J W c	A	Clyde
Kelley Wesley B	C	Densmore
Knapp Geo W	C	South Haven
Longston Perry C c	C	Palmer
Mann W H	K	Kill Creek
Martin J S	B	Girard
McCoy Robt s	F	Cawker City
McMurphy A	A	Sterling
Neff Isaac	D	Glen Elder
Parker J M	F	Burrton
Porter L H	A	Fredonia
Patterson Wm	C	Alton
Piety A H capt	G	Topeka
Piercy Philip s	C	Iuka
Pratt J B	H	Emporia
Ralts O N c	M	Douglas
Reed J M s	L	Burrton
Ricketts J M	K	Byron
Ryan L	G	Hope
Sheets Edwin s	L	Palmer
Sizemore Abijah c	A	Coyville
Skinner W M s	E	Gaylord
Striker Jacob	E	Fredonia
Waymire W	G	Dexter
Wells S H c	G	Dexter
Williams C M	G	Connors
Williams J M c	A	Washington
Young J A	G	Rose
Zook I K	B	Yates Center

ONE HUNDRED AND TWENTIETH INFANTRY, THREE YEARS REGIMENT.

Colonels—R. F. Baxter, Allen W. Prother, Reuben C. Kise.

Name	Co.	Place
Allen Wm M c	D	N Topeka
Boggs Lewis	K	Manhattan
Brown W W	A	Arkansas City
Buck G W	B	Climax
Burkdoff G F	F	Lyndon
Cochran C M c	D	Mt Hope
Cornett W H	H	Toronto
Cummings J P lt	H	Minneapolis
Dixon W S	K	Oak Wood
Ellis John c	C	Manc
Garten J W	D	Solomon
Garten G W	D	Solomon
Gilbam Henry Capt	C	Oswego

Harris C A c	C	Iola
Harrison R G	asst surg	Frankfort
Hennings C B	G	Sedan
Higgins A P	H	Hutchinson
Hinds S O	H	Lincoln
Howe J W 1st s	A	Independence
Houston J L	A	Dexter
King Elijah c	C	Paola
Laughlin Robt	D	Haven
Lutes Geo M c	H	Lincoln
Mayfield Isaac	hosp steward	Randolph
McCammon F M	K	Oxford
McClaskey I R 1st s	B	Wellington
Moore I J	G	Mound Valley
Morgan M W	E	Olathe
Plunket J M lt	C	Holton
Ramey D E c	H	Cedarvale
Spear E A	B	Clay Center
Stanfield G W	H	Manhattan
Stanfield R T	K	Republic
Sumpter John R c	H	Tannehill
Sweeny J H	K	Jewell
Tobias G E	K	LaMont
West Elnathan c	B	Humboldt
Willis W B	G	Howard
Wilson W P lt	K	Barton
Wray C H c	B	Hutchinson

ONE HUNDRED AND TWENTY-FIRST REGI-
MENT, NINTH CAVALRY, THREE
YEARS.

Cols. Wm. S. McClure, George W. Jackson, Eli Lilly.

Allen Wm	D	Concordia
Allen J M	D	Wichita
Almond J K	I	Media
Baker H	M	Hutchinson
Ballard Cornelius c	I	Silver Lake
Bell A	C	Lawrence
Bickford W M surg		Florence
Brown Finley	D	Mound Valley
Burden John	I	Grenola
Clements Reuben	I	Emporia
Christ C W s	I	Wichita
Edwards J L	E	Earlton
Elkenberry Andrew	D	Conway
Epler Isaac S	A	Prescott
Fish T J	K	Peabody
Fisk Othniel	B	Madison
Frounfelter D	L	Burden
Garris J E	E	Garnett
Goldsberry T W	H	Columbus
Gwinn Ezekiel	E	Humboldt
Harris A B 1st s	B	Pomona
Hardin Wm H	H	Marysville
Himes James	A	Roscoe
Howard Wm	C	Emporia
Jackson G W c		New Salem
Kiger Mathias	B	Pittsburg
King S W	I	Harper
Kirkpatrick N	G	Lyndon
LaBar J W c	M	Monroe
Lane John	G	Ottumwa
Langston A	D	Clifford
Mercer R	E	Clifton
Patterson Edward	L	Cloverdale
Pert V N	I	Wetmore
Pratt Geo W	E	Lyons
Ratcliff John	E	Chester, Neb
Roe Samuel	C	Dorrance

Sanford G C	D	Sabetha
Spradling J G	G	Veitsburg
Stewart Thos B	L	Elk City
Thornburg B	C	Long Island
Thornburg S M	C	Eskridge
Turner H	L	LeRoy
Windhorst J	K	Washington
Wilborn M V	B	Iola
Woodring P D c	G	Coffeyville
Work E M	F	Liberty
Wright W B s	G	Topeka

ONE HUNDRED AND TWENTY-SECOND REGIMENT.—Not Organized.

ONE-HUNDRED AND TWENTY-THIRD INFANTRY, THREE YEARS' REGIMENT.

Colonel, John C McQuiston.

Avery Wm A	B	Spearville
Barber Z S	E	Hutchinson
Brower A H	D	Gaylord
Bruner David	C	Fontana
Burley Joshua	F	Ottawa
Burt Wm W c	K	Severy
Connard John 1st s	D	Mission Creek, Neb
Davidson John lt	B	Waushara
Downs Howard	C	Tonganoxie
Duninger D W	H	Caldwell
Ewart A J s	B	Topeka
Fetter Fred H	K	Lawrence
Garyer J H'	A	Council Grove
Glenn J W 1st lt	I	Sedan
Gray Geo R	G	Chester
Helms Andrew s	I	Silve Lake
Hollis J C s	H	Pelphos
Jones Milo C	K	La Cygne
Keely Samuel L	G	Winfield
Kersey J H	D	Judson
Lewis Isaac	H	Galena
Lucas Hagan	B	Xenia
McNutt James	K	North Branch
Myers A J	G	Udall
Nelson James	B	Cheney
Nichols J J	C	Fall River
Paramore J A L	A	Tipton
Faris L A	F	Garnett
Porter W M c	D	Mulvane
Reese James M	K	Kingman
Reeves Caleb L	F	Chanute
Richter H E c	I	Council Grove
Risk Abisha	A	St. John
Sands Jacob c	A	Vining
Simpson Wm	A	Canton
Sparks R H chaplain		Columbus
Stephenson Wm	B	LaCygne
Thorpe Robert	B	Winfield
Ventel Rosel	H	Chetopa

ONE HUNDRED AND TWENTY-FOURTH INFANTRY—THREE YEARS' REG'T.

Cols—James Burgess, John M Orr.

Adams S L c	H	Anthony
Arnold G W s	G	Newton
Bales John R	G	Burt
Burgess James	Colonel	N Topeka
Bush Martin S 1st lt	A	Blaine
Canfield Geo c	A	Kansas City
Carver Michael s	B	Altoona
Cope J R	I	Harper

Dick F M c   B   Sedgewick City
Dilworth Chas E   C   Guelph
Ellis John T   K   Warrentown
England John   C   Garnett
Fisher W W fifer   E   Tiblow
Fleishman J G   E   Dodge City
Gordon B F   G   Finney
Hart John H   H   Sedgewick
Hilligoss A C   A   Sedan
Hyten Wm T c   D   Ewell
Keefer H C   B   Harper
Lamb Geo W   K   Paola
Manle Chare I c   F   Strong City
Mallenor Fred   F   Chetopa
Pollock John T   A   Bulls City
Pumphrey A J   I   Nickerson
Stoneyfield H c   C   Guilford
Sinex C A c   K   Peabody
Slagle D C c   C   Ionia
Small G W   D   Mission Creek
StephensC C lt   F   Walnut
Statesman S   D   Metz

ONE HUNDRED TWENTY-FIFTH REGIMENT, TENTH CAVALRY—THREE YEARS.

Cols—Thos N. Page, Geo R. Swallow.

Armstrong R   M   Peabody
Ball L T W   C   Beloit
Cody B G q m s   L   Wellsville
Bramwell Joseph   H   Pretty Prairie
Carlton Gabriel W   I   Derby
Carlton David M   I   Darby
Chambers A E   H   Clearwater
Cheshire J A s   L   Emporia
Clark Charnal   M   Toronto
Fivecoat M   L   Hadcam
Goodell Willis   E   Melvern
Higginbotham J G c B   Neodesha
Hughes S E   H   Ottumwa
Hulse John A   L • Cottonwood Falls
Jones J F   F   Beaumont
Land A B   H   Ridgeway
Lansbury J E   L   Matfield Green
Lick A C   H   Ft Scott
Lovett Chas G   B   Neodesha
McCausland D 1st s   C   Gaylord
McKinney Joseph   A   El Dorado
Morris Wm 1st lt   G   Caldwell
Niemohler H   M   Wakefield
O'Rourke John   A   Strong City
Pering C C s   I   Abilene
Patrick Daniel   C   Leonardville
Walters T A   B   Clay Center
Warner W C   B   Warnertown
Whelshel C B   I   Saronsburg
Young Geo F   I   N Topeka

ONE HUNDRED AND TWENTY-SIXTH REGIMENT—ELEVENTH CAVALRY, THREE YEARS.

Colonels, Robt. R. Stewart, Abram Sharra.

Abbott J H c   I   Baxter Springs
Bayles John N   D   LeRoy
Blackwell R D   H   Douglas
Blalock W R   G   Elk Falls
Barnhardt J W   C   Widerange
Brown W L   E   Sabetha
Burr J H c   Waverly
Carrington lt   I   Burlington
Cartright Thomas s G   Neodesha

Name		Location
Catick J C qm	K	N Topeka
Chambers Joseph	B	Howard
Chambers W B	L	Pratt
Coy W L	E	Council Grove
Crisman Robt	F	Ashland
Christ Geo W 1st s	I	Topeka
Cruthard A	E	Augusta
Culbison J W s	B	Mankato
Currant Thos	B	Howard
Doster A F c	M	Marion
Ellis E T	L	Atchison
Ellis T H	I	Chanute
Fisher David	E	Leavenworth
Garrison S	L	Urbana
Givens W B capt	M	Leavenworth
Goodale Jude c	C	Pawnee Rock
Gourley Thos	I	Topeka
Griggs L T s	A	Atchison
Hadley Wm	L	Sedan
Hamilton John W	M	Marion
Hammon Taylor	C	Scandia
Harrison Jay L	K	Media
Haworth I M	L	Iga
Hitchcock J W c	I	Peabody
Harper R C lt	B	Independence
Hull Jerome	H	Matfield Green
James C K s	K	Hardy, Neb
James R M	K	Republic
Kelley D J s	B	Concordia
Kerns Thos D	B	Howard
Loughton Chas	M	Sterling
Lamb Wm	K	Girard
Ledman A M s	M	Elk City
LeMaster E c	E	Ottawa
Magill J A c	K	Buffalo
Mapes Joel B c	A	Ft Scott
Maries C E s	L	Farmersburg
McDowell S O	M	Columbus or Topeka
McIntyre A W q m s	G	Neosho Falls
Miller Albion E	M	Crestline
Mooney Robt s	G	New Albany
Monroe A J	L	Lyons
Mull C G	F	Carlyle
Mullendore John	M	Smithfield Mo
Myers A J s	C	Robinson
O'Rear R F	G	Independence
Osborn Robt c	E	Ft Scott
Overbeck Wm c	D	Mahone
Patterson J L	L	Burlington
Paugh R S	K	Bronson
Reed J B	H	Jewell City
Rice Abijah	E	Kingman
Rorey Joseph	E	Dunlap
Ross R W	L	Andover
Russell W H	I	Douglas
Sanders D L	B	Mankato
Sherman T	H	Burlingame
Stephenson J A capt	K	Hutchinson
Swank D	K	Canton
Swank J F	K	Cottonwood Falls
Taylor H	F	Pittsburg
Thompson L	M	Chanute
Tuttle N P	F	London
White H	A	Kingman
Wier R A	G	Parsons
Winans S	C	Ladore
Wright E A	L	Wichita
Wunsh F	D	Atchison
Woung Y H	D	Concordia

ONE HUNDRED AND TWENTY SEVENTH REGIMENT, TWELFTH CAVALRY, THREE YEARS.

Colonel, Edward Anderson.

Name	Co.	Residence
Abdell A E	H	Rossville, Lawrence
Asher James H	A	Greeley
Baker Tim R capt	B	Avon
Benter D M 1st s	I	Parsons
Bemmer J S	M	Jonesburg
Bissell Wm 1st lt	M	Phillipsburg
Bolin Daniel	I	Climax
Bags Charles	G	Grenola
Briggs G W	M	Madison
Brooks L	G	Peru
Brown E D	K	Newton
Burnett E C 1st s	L	Parsons
Crapp Uriah	K	Roxbury
Clowes D A ass't s	G	Armistead
Cruzan W M	E	Ft Scott
Curtis Andrew	H	Ottawa
Dressler D N lt	H	Winfield
Duncan C N com s	L	Topeka
Dyer J N	A	Parsons
Ellis A A	M	Tonganoxie
Farrall John	G	Chatauqua
Fee Nathan H	I	Bala or Gatesville
Francis R H	E	Hubbell
Geiger John II	L	Concordia
Haggerty James H	I	Oswego
Hendricks C N s	A	Wellington
Johnson F T 1st lt	B	Eimdale
Jones W H c	E	Miami
Jones Giles A	M	Westmoreland
Kelley Noah s	K	Vining
Kephart Henry c	K	Big Springs
Kious J M		Meridian
Le Master E	E	Ottawa
Livengood C E capt	D	Alta
Lownman J C s	I	Oxford
Manwarren Geo s	C	Lyons
Mercer Rufus	E	Clifton
Miller Silas H	F	Grenola
Morrow Josiah s	H	Mankato
Nafus Daniel M	G	Parsons
Nash Marvin	G	Moline
Nuttle James W	I	Wilson
Owens Geo K	L	Altoona
Peters Henry	G	Rates Center
Pinkerton John	E	Lincoln
Preston Levi H	I	Greenleaf
Ridenour Jas s	L	Arkansas City
Sanders J T s	G	Wellington
Scritchfield W T	G	West Moreland
Settle J D	D	Belleville
Snodgrass J M	E	Stuart
Stoddard Sheldon	M	Kansas Center
Story S S	B	Lebanon
Story W G	B	Milford or Bala
Taggart D	L	Emporia
Tincher Geo c	A	N Topeka
Truitt Adam c	K	Elk City
Taylor Geo W	K	Kirwin
Weed John	G	Burlington
Williams D E lt	A	Iola
Wilson J Y	F	Kingman
Wykoff C	C	Bigelow

ONE HUNDRED AND TWENTY-EIGHTH INFANTRY, THREE YEARS.

Colonels, R. P. De Hart, Jasper Packard

Aubert Anton	D	St Marys
Avery Wm H	D	Grover
Ball Robt G	G	Eureka
Bell Jonathon	A	Marion
Blessing Joseph lt	A	Fame
Branner A W c	C	Adams Peak
Bridgeman J O c	I	Salt Creek
Buchtel Wm	D	Cawker City
Burdge John s	K	N Topeka
Cissne R M	C	Uniontown
Cleghorn D	H	Longton
Coho B R C	D	Effingham
Foltz G W	G	Peru
Freeman W S	B	Harper
Frieze John	A	Jewell
Fuller Benj O s	H	Little River
Garver J A	K	Melvern
Glasgow E B q m s	A	Olivet
Gregory Joseph	H	Haworth or Cuba
Harris Geo W c	H	Oak Valley
Haskell G K lt	A	Bodock
Hathaway Daniel	D	Burlington
Hickman J A c	G	Marion
Houston R c	B	Cherryvale
Johnson J F	B	Burlingame
Kauffman J	K	Rossville
Krieder A B c	D	Westphalia
Liggert Wm A c	D	Kingman
Marshall J B s	C	Olathe
McLaughlin T J	K	N Topeka
McJunkins A	E	Stuart
Morris J L	A	Scio
Myers D A	F	Michigan Valley
Mock Daniel	H	Spring Valley
Nichols John	G	Wellington
Nichols B F c	H	Ost
Plants Jacob C 1st s	C	Rosalia
Pottenger J M c	I	Chetopa
Reynolds J	A	Altoona
Ritter John F c	H	Asherville
Robinson G E	E	Belle Plaine
Rowe J M	D	Conway
Russell A J	K	Lyons
Shuman Jacob	K	Saratoga
Thompson L R	G	Partis
Thoroughman J H	I	Yates Center
Toms Harvey c	H	Burlington
Ward Charles	F	Amer
Whitaker N	B	Gardner

ONE HUNDRED AND TWENTY-NINTH INFANTRY—THREE YEARS.

Colonels—Charles Case, Ch A. Zolliger.

Amrine J M	F	Jewell City
Crouse Geo W	K	Augusta
Crone Henry c	K	Sedgwick
Day J D		Stanton
Dickey Joseph C capt	D	Waterville
Fowler Stephen s	I	Halstead
Freeby J H	H	Barnes
Fruit Adam	K	Sedan
Green John C m	G	Reynolds
Greenamyre John	H	Mona
Hammond John S	G	Bunker Hill
Leard S F c	B	Canton

McClary John	G	Marion
McClure James F s	B	Gaylord
McConohay A A c	K	Howard
Overstreet J	G	Garnett
Reynolds W H	E	Custer
Rogers A L	B	LeRoy
Shatto I N	A	Butler
Shaw D W	K	Pittsburg
Squires J W	F	Wyandotte
Stephenson J W		Peabody
Strong B F c	D	Independence
Sultz Isaac c	G	Fellsburg
Trisket Leo	A	Abilene
Walker J R	K	Minneapolis

ONE HUNDRED THIRTIETH INFANTRY

THREE YEARS.

Colonel—Charles S. Parrish.

Adamson J	K	Sunnydale
Adams J	K	Mona
Barrett Stephen	E	Allegan
Becker Abram	D	Quenemo
Butcher A P	A	Wichita
Cook M O	B	Fontana
Dilley Isaac	H	Rule, Neb
England James	B	Eli
Hackney A L	I	Parsons
Hall Isaac	K	Barton
Harpole Sam'l	B	Conway Springs
Harris E	C	Emporia
Jones Damson	K	Stanton
Jones O V L c	K	Sedan
Landes H F	H	Wellington
Makepence E A	B	Augusta
Mason Sylvanus	D	Center Ridge
Moon Isaac C	F	Concordia
Nave Wesley	D	South Haven
Newhouse Albert c	K	Burr Oak
O'Leary Francis	D	Everest
Pattison G W	surgeon	Cleveland
Pfaff J H	C	Wilburn
Ratliff Eli	H	Iola
Richards Ellwood A	A	Sterling
Rivers Peter	E	Piedmont
Rude H B	I	Burden
Russey Mc K	I	Parsons
Reoger John lt	E	Kingman
Scott Winfield 1st s	C	Norway
Smith Wm s	K	Independence
Sowers A H	D	Paw Paw
Swaldner M	D	Center Ridge
Taylor S S	H	Toronto
Ward John	F	Silver Lake
Watkins W P 1st s	B	Anthony
Wayman J M s	H	Hutchinson

ONE HUNDRED AND THIRTY-FIRST REGIMENT, THIRTEENTH CAVALRY,

THREE YEARS.

Col. Gilbert M. L. Johnson.

Adams J A	A	Wilson
Biggs Jeremiah s	G	Chanute
Blount J J	A	Topsy
Beauchamp W	A	Troy
Bradford O A bugler	A	Topeka
Brandenberg S S	F	Harper
Burns Geo c	G	Independence
Carpenter LaFayette bugler	G	Galesburg

Conrad Jacob H	capt	D	Liberty
Conwell A L		A	Oneida
Copeland Uriah	c	F	Winfield
Crandall R N		F	Newton
Davis H C	c	D	Dodge City
Doolittle O R		G	Galesburg
Edwards Thos S		H	Ottawa
Ferris John	s	M	Lecompton
Hamacher W H	c	M	Eureka
Herman Jacob	capt	B	Elk City
Harrison C C		F	Topeka
Harris J M		K	Saratoga
Hendricks T		D	West Plains
Houseman G W		A	Ellis
Jarboe W T		L	Wellington
Kephart Henry	o	K	Big Springs
Lockhart G W	c	E	Kingman
Long Wm H		K	Dennis
Lahue C J		D	Kinsley
Maddox J C		A	Topeka
Matchett J R		H	Paris
Miller Daniel		A	Lawrence
Moore Scatt	s	K	Cherryvale
Muth H K	chaplain		Ottawa
Owens Thomas		F	Eureka
Pulse S A	lt	A	Walton
Playton Benj		C	Burns
Powers B		H	Mankato
Priddy Joseph W		A	North Topeka
Rich Elias			Burlington
Roderick L A	s	M	Troy
Rosenberry P W		I	Mt Carmel
Shockley Jacob		G	North Topeka
Simmons J J	c	F	Pleasanton
Sinclair John		A	Cloverdale
Stockslager T A	s	L	Columbus
Stricker Lewis	s	C	Topeka
Sumner J		L	Ft Scott
Taylor Wm M		G	Lyons
Taylor H		F	Pittsburg
Terry G F	s	K	Marietta
Timberlake W H	s maj		Columbus
Vallance F J		A	Plumb
Watkins D K	s	K	Lane
Weir D L	s	M	Wellington
Wills J W	s	D	Waverly
Wolf C CW	s	M	Ozark

THE ONE HUNDRED DAYS VOLUNTEERS.

The Governors of Ohio, Indiana, Illinois, Iowa and Wisconsin having offered to raise for the service of the General Government a force of volunteers to serve for 100 days, Governor Morton on the 23d of April, 1864, issued his call for Indiana's proportion of that force. The troops thus raised were to perform such military services as might be required of them in any state, and were to be armed, subsisted, clothed and paid by the United States, but were not to receive any bounty.

These troops were designed to aid in making the campaign of 1864 successful and decisive, by relieving a large number o veterans from garrison and guard duty, and allow them to join their companions in arms, then about entering upon one of the r active and important campaigns of the war. Their places were filled by the 100 days men as fast as the latter could be organized into regiments and sent forward from the camps of rendezvous. The organizations from Indiana consisted of eight regiments, numbered consecutively from the 132d to the 139th inclusive.

ONE HUNDRED AND THIRTY SECOND INFANTRY, ONE HUNDRED DAYS REGIMENT.

Col. Samuel C. Vance.

Anderson C	C	Beloit
Bartelow O W	K	Lyle
Branham O	B	Winfield or Ark's City
Branch N G s	G	Paola
Brunnimos J O	G	Jewell
Bright W R	B	Longton
Dixon John E	A	White Rock
Duncan J W	H	Humboldt
Eastburn Wm H	G	Independence
Fletcher I J	A	Wyandotte
Foss Wm		Newton
Givens Wm L	C	Augusta
Guthrie S W	D	Barton
Hamilton J M	G	Independence
Hill Levi D	G	Salina
Lowe James H	G	Osawkee
Mantz Wesley	C	Melvern
Maferty J W	C	Big Springs
Maze J T c	E	Topeka or N Topeka
Miller E S	G	Iola
Riggon J W	H	Clifford
Rutherford Wm	G	Howard
Sargent L W m	K	Lyndon
Stagg Wm J	D	Topeka
Tilford D W	B	Cheney
Turner Moses	H	Cresson
Vaughn L C	H	Bellville
West W C	G	Beloit

ONE HUNDRED AND THIRTY-THIRD INFANTRY, ONE HUNDRED DAYS REGIMENT.

Col. Robert N. Hudson.

Allen Robert N	F	Chanute
Alward Ira	G	Brooks
Andrews A N	I	Yale
Arnold Aug lt	H	Dodge City
Brown W L	E	Sabetha
Bostwick D W	G	Iola
Burnett Wm c	H	Council Grove
Chessman W	G	Sweet Home
Collier John	E	Sutphens Mill
Cruthers F	K	Climax
Dicks Nathan S	F	Ottawa
Dowdell Joseph S s	G	North Topeka
Elliot James W	H	Yates Center
Hanks H	H	Sterling
Harris A L	A	Emporia
Kent Isaac	K	Clyde
Killion Enos	B	Lorena
Kuhn E N	G	Lawrence
Laughlin Eli	K	Altamont
Lyons Wm D	G	Richland or Scranton
Manker Lewis s	B	Topeka
McCutchan W F	G	Richmond
Miller J N c	A	Caldwell
Nordyke S A	A	Wyandotte
...ed M J	B	Marion

Shipley J A	G	Burlingame
Stoddard C H	D	Erie
Story W c	E	Attica
Uselman A S	C	Prescott
Whitcanack B	H	Oak Valley

ONE HUNDRED AND THIRTY-FOURTH IN-
FANTRY, ONE HUNDRED DAYS
REGIMENT.

Colonel, James Gavin.

Allender W H	K	Axtell
Baker Cris	J	Boston Mills
Buchanan A G 1st s	E	Abilene
Caldwell J D	E	Wichita
Campbell C W m	A	Topeka
Cappen Wm	D	Somerset
Conrad H W c	E	Independence
Danner T J	E	Spring Hill
Deffenbaugh D o	G	Ashland
Dowd Albert	K	Ft Scott
Dogget David	D	Girard
Fiscus Marion	B	Eldorado
Friendly W M 1st lt	E	West Plains
Fuedline M H	A	Fredonia
Glaze James	G	Girard
Glenn James	C	Iola
Grubbs R E	F	Arkansas City
Hinman L M c	E	Huntsville
Hughes A E	H	Topeka
Hungate A J capt	K	Topeka
Junkens J H	K	Cherokee
Knight James	E	Garnett
Marsh Wm T capt	E	Topeka
Merideth F M	D	Eskridge
Merideth Wm	D	Eskridge
Parson S B	A	Arkansas City
Parson Geo	C	Garnett
Risinger Joseph	C	Fredonia
Roland O F	E	Oxford
Shidler J S	G	Harveyville
Silver J R capt	K	Topeka
Smawley H B 1st s	B	Erie
Steele James C	F	Howard
Valentine J C	I	Effingham
Webb T F	H	Monroe
Wyatt Isaac	K	Severy
Zeigler Wm M	E	Hays City

ONE HUNDRED AND THIRTY FIFTH IN-
FANTRY, ONE HUNDRED DAYS
REGIMENT.

Colonel—Wm C. Wilson.

Antrim Edom	B	Cleveland
Ballinger Wm	G	Lucas
Blankenship Wm c	B	Rosalia
Boyd John L chaplain		Wichita
Burroughs B C	A	Kingman
Elrod Geo W	F	Edgerton
Ferguson J C	H	Twin Falls
Haynes W L c	B	Topeka
Holmes C J c	K	Gaylord
James F A	D	Manhattan
Johnson Wm W	B	Girard
Leatherman A S	C	Clyde
McFarland John	D	Cherokee
Miller John	B	Melvern
Monitor J	K	Newton

Moore R H	B	Wheatland
Mount J	C	Hillsdale
Owens J W	B	Coyville
Pallett Henry	D	Coffeyville
Scribner N O	E	Caldwell
Snodgrass W H	I	L ttle River
Stont Wilson	F	Cottonwood Falls
Taylor W H m	D	Wellington
Wagoner I J	K	Independence
Waymire H	F	Yates Center
Yonkey J	F	Alexander

ONE HUNDRED AND THIRTY-SIXTH IN-FANTRY, ONE HUNDRED DAYS REGIMENT.

Colonel—John W Foster.

Abney Elisha N	D	Oswego
Bain W S	B	I la
Cook W H	D	Fontana
Cupps Caleb	H	Haven
Farley T P lt	B	Valley Falls
Gilbert John	D	Deerton
Gould Wm K	K	Elm Valley
Green E S	H	Chanute
Grimes S H	K	Marion
Grosse Sol	I	Russell
Harrold E	E	Paola
Morgan John c	I	Buffalo Park
Short W E pr	H	Fredonia
Urie Geo A	B	Carbondale
Young A G	I	Cottonwood Falls

ONE HUNDRED AND THIRTY SEVENTH IN-FANTRY, ONE-HUNDRED DAYS REGIMENT.

Colonel—Edward J. Robinson.

Alley Tilman H	D	Cedarvale
Anderson W H		Winchester
Brown H C	K	Independence
Brundridge J	E	Olathe
Chamberlin W B lt	K	Humboldt
Childs H B	K	Walton
Childs O L	K	Walton
Dawes Isaac B s	E	Miltonvale
Day J D lt	B	Stanton
Fifer Sam	C	Burr Oak
Finney Andrew	D	Cottonwood Falls
Foster Sames s	E	Abilene
Fouts Thos D lt col		Wichita
Graham J M	B	Florence
Harris T G	F	Edna
Horseman John	C	Council Grove
Jennings J S	G	Wichita
Jones Geo	C	Allegan
Larew A J	I	Burlington
Madden T	F	Bridge
Merrill Geo	F	Topeka
McConnell J C	A	Carbondale
Powers J D	F	Topeka
Robertson W S	G	Eureka
Roop James R	A	Everest
Sauders I H	B	Osakee
Sewell L	E	Clay Center
Sherman M	H	Altamont
Simons Enos	E	Mulberry Grove
Stagg W J	I	Topeka
Walton Columbus	A	Clay Center
Wilson A D	B	Scandia
Wilson Scott	D	Arkansas City

ONE HUNDRED AND THIRTY EIGHTH IN-
FANTRY, ONE HUNDRED DAYS
REGIMENT.
Col—James H. Shannon.

Cruzan Wm h	K	Newton
Fisher Geo W c	A	Topeka
Gasney A W	H	Burlington
Grant John c	E	Howard
Green A J	H	Rubens
Hammer H	I	Lincoln
Hilderly David	C	Onaga
Huffman H	E	Larned
Keagle G W	G	Pittsburg
Kehler H B	G	Solomon
Morley J B c	D	Moline
Mullinour G W	E	Chetopa
Oliver W H	H	Thayer
Register Robt	B	Lenora
Roach S C	H	Milan
Rodgers A K	K	Topeka
Root Sam'l	F	Elk Falls
Russel Frank	G	Oneida
Short W T	E	Concordia
Speere Edward	C	Manhattan
Street Thomas	C	Keelville
Swartz E K c	I	St John
Underwood T W	H	Hutchinson
Winfield S	F	Chanute
Wherrett I N capt	G	Veitsburg

ONE HUNDRED AND THIRTY-NINTH IN-
FANTRY, ONE HUNDRED DAYS
REGIMENT.
Col—George Humphrey.

Anderson J S c	E	Winfield
Edmundson G W	G	Ottawa
Erwin L M	A ·	Millerton
Forsha M	D	Hardilee
Gordon A W 2d lt	H	Abilene
Greenfield C W	C	Burrton
Hall Lewis D	I	Concordia
Hall L N	A	Ohio
Johnston Theo	I	Neodesha
Kuhlman Enos	H	Arkansas City
Loofborrow P S	I	Clay Center
McHenry P F	B	Melvern
McIntosh J G	F	Gale
Mills Barney	D	Greeley
Moore Geo	K	Garden City
Nixon S E	G	Big Springs
Rising D T	I	Lebo
Roberts James	E	Hallowell
Rogers John D	A	Mound Valley
Sutton G W capt	C	Hartford
Taylor Sam'l	C	Havensville
Taylor J S	C	Lura
Thompson J B c	C	Melvern
Weaver C B 1st s	K	Everest
West G T	I	Plum Grove

ONE HUNDRED AND FORTIETH INFANTRY
ONE YEaRS' SERVICE.
Colonel— Thomas J. Brady.

Alley Lorenzo D	G	Farlinville
Anderson T J	K	Arkansas City
Arment J A	H	Dodge City
Blum Protus	B	Buffalo
Bond E W lt	F	Girard
Bowman Wm	E	Coffeyville

Name		Co.		Place
Bright Dan R		H		Norton
Chrisman G W		F		Wyandotte
Cole John W		B		Chanute
Cole Doctor J		I		Saratoga
Cole Charles M	B	Center Ridge or Rolla
Darbrow Edward		A		Neodesha
Dowell Geo W		D		Blue Mound
Ebright Philip c		C		Covet
Green Elias S	s A		Clements or Wanseon
Griffith Tutman		G		Belvue
Howey John L		K		Arkansas City
Kriete Henry		I		Burrton
McGregor T B	1st lt	B		Melvern
Miller Elijah		A		Montana
Minton Joseph	c	C		Anthony
Mitchell D T		A		Wichita
Mitchell D T	lt col			Wichita
Myers Isaac J		F		Dun
Montgomery N C	c A			Burlington
Nelson J M				Caldwell
Oram J W		I		Great Bend
Patterson J H	c	D		Plainville
Piatt W C	asst surg			Plainville
Silver W F		B		Winfield
Sizemore L		F		Greely
Smith J L		G		Baesettville
Snyder Dan'l		G		Moline
Sturnes G W		E		Wichita
Stryker C W		D		Mound Valley
Sweany Olliver		D		Vining
Sweezy W C	surg			Olivet
Trego John		C		Topeka
Tuttle John W		C		Peabody
Umbarger W H		E		Oswego
Van Horn W M	s	F		Galena
Weddles N S	lt	K		King City
Wills Robert		C		Scandia
Wood Perry		D		Hymer
Young A G		A		Ottawa

ONE HUNDRED AND FORTY–FIRST INDIANA
INFANTRY.

Authorized, but not organized.

ONE HUNDRED AND FORTY-SECONN IN-
FANTRY ONE YEARS SERVICE.

Col. John M. Comparet.

Name		Co.		Place
Baldwin W S		K		Green
Barber D J		G		Ashland
Benjamin J	c	B		Pomona
Bloomhuff F M		E		Emporia
Breeze E J		F		Scammonville
Bruce Jesse		B		Uniontown
Chaffee J R		A		Randolph
Cooper V R		G		Greenleaf
Craig Amos		K		Elwood
Daniels A		F		Norton
Driver Isaiah		A		Sterling
Dye Harvey		G		State Center
Fink Michael		I		Burris
Foywell S		G		Grand Haven
Grisley P M		C		Meriden
Hall W N		I		Sterling
Hollinger C C		F		Newton
Houdyshell S		G		Lyons
Johnson Charles	c K			Woodville
Logan J B		H		Marysville
Loucks Peter B		D		Newton
McFarland J	1st lt	H		Cherryvale

Payton M C c	H	Scranton or Durlingame
Rakestraw C	I	Sterling
Riggs C T	K	Medicine Lodge
Rogers A K s	B	Topeka
Rogers A T	B	Top.
Shannon C F s	C	Kingman
Sims Geo W	I	Chase
Swan R W capt	F	Newton
Williamson L	B	Topeka
Wolverton A B m	D	Topeka
Wood M C	K	Goddard
Winbigler J L	B	Oswego

ONE HUNDRED AND FORTY-THIRD INFAN-TRY, ONE YEAR'S SERVICE.

Col. John F. Grill.

Bidwell A J	F	Mulvane
Bryant Eli D	H	Wichita
Burress G W	K	Emporia
Fickas F W capt	E	Carbondale
House Chas	C	Paola
Houseley Wm c	I	Independence
Puett Wm J 1st lt	D	. Newton
Rogers J T	I	Benton
Smith Geo F	B	Gorham
Trueblood Jas	K	Finney
Trueblood H S c	K	Yates Center
Schmuck Peter capt		Hunds Station
Worthington E R s	F	Densmore
White H	F	Pawnee

ONE HUNDRED AND FORTY-FOURTH IN-FANTRY, ONE YEAR'S SERVICE.

Colonel—Geo W Riddle.

Bachelder I S	I	Fredonia
Cook A	E	Dodge City
Conn A	H	Glasco
Custer N V c	H	Peru
Dilman G W	D	Padonia
Dellano W H	C	Hutchinson
Green W M s	C	Rest
Hopson Thomas	K	Lura
Hunter J H	I	Bross
Jones Wm	F	Frankfort
Janes Joseph H	H	Hutchinson
Lindsay J		Topeka
McCartney J A	D	WaKeeney
McCory Josiah	B	Raymond
Miller B F	I	Mound Valley
Morris L M c	C	Scandia
Nichols S T	I	Wyandotte
Poe Ira	D	Floral
Sappenfield R s	F	Milan
Snider John	E	Kiowa
Stanton H T	H	Piqua
Tower Z T	H	Leeds
Woods Isaac c	F	Oxford
Zimmerman A J	E	Bennington
Zink T J	C	Hartford

ONE HUNDRED FORTY-FIFTH INFANTRY, ONE YEAR'S SERVICE.

Colonel—Will A. Adams

Bevis John H	H	Great Bend
Butcher James s	C	Soldier
Campbell J M s	B	Manshara
Collings Isaac	G	Jordon Springs
Curry James F s	E	Eskridge

Dougherty W M capt F Cedarvale
Drake B F H Sev ry
Durham Geo H capt A Kan City, Kan
Everhart C S C Pliny
Grant Reuben F Minneapolis
Graham Elijah K Edmond
Gross Solomon D Russell
Haney J T C Minneapolis
Hess James F Neosho Falls
Hornbaker F D I Newton
Hornbaker J M I Newton
Hostetetler J W B Lina
Hudiburg Thos mu K Burr Oak
Hunter Mahlon 2d lt E Arkansas City
Kirtley Wm F H Arkansas City
Keith J W E Manhattan
Light Joseph H 1st s C Chanute
Long John L B Thayer
Markwell J A H A Newton
Meek W H I Osage City
Miller G W lt F Salina
Murphy T J G Stockdale
Nelson Geo K Litchfield
Pond James O B Thayer
Robinson E C capt C Fredonia
Rogers Jonathan C Floral
Roudebush C L G Great Bend
Sypes B A B Pleasanton
Smith Joseph I Cambridge
Smith J T G Hutchinson
Sipes P A B Reece
Stanfield H G Stockdale
Sturt John c H Cherryvale
Taylor A M F State Center
Thompson N R A Williamsburg
Weddle D C F King City
Wilson Sam'l F Holmwood
Winters J M E La Harpe

ONE HUNDRED FORTY-SIXTH INFANTRY
ONE YEAR'S SERVICE.

Colonel—Merit C. Welch.

Baldwin W J C Topeka
Baxter J H c F Columbus
Carnine W J D Norton
Craig J M asst uorg Baxter Springs
De Moss C M drummer F Beattie
Dunn Andrew H E Paola
Duree James H N Topeka
Graham J W D Florence
Keeler Thos c F Soldier or Sandago
Lovell James G I Shibboleth
McCord J R C Stilson
Morgan David c I Vermillion
Reed Geo R A Columbus
Reed T N A Severy
Seeds Geo W c G Lansing
Simmons Philip B Strawberry
Sweetman J P C Sterling
Truitt J F E Laura
Taylor J L I Lura
Turner B F Salina
Whetsel M V F Peabody
Wagoner A A A Burlington
Wyatt John D Independence

ONE HUNDRED FORTY SEVENTH INFANTRY,
ONE YEAR'S SERVICE.

Colonel — Milton Peden.

Alfred J W	H	Pratt
Bailey F J S	A	Yates Center
Boothe James A	K	Girard
Bowers David	H	Sedgewick
Butts Moses C c		La Cygne
Cooper John E	D	Ida
Corn Charles F c	B	Morehead
Cloud Joseph	G	Hesper
Darter Alex	B	Douglas
Dougherty Jasper	E	El Dorado
Deer Job	E	Harrisonville
Dickey M B capt	I	Richland
Dille Geo J	H	Vermillion
Ellison J	C	Chautauqua Springs
Engle Wm R	G	Dexter
Fye Charles	I	Oak Valley
Good Abraham	C	Farlington
Heaton Newton	C	Whiting
Kiser Geo W	F	Iola
Lewis C D c	I	Concordia
Massey Francis	A	Topeka
Madden John	F	Cottonwood Falls
Null Wm F	F	Osage Mission
Pestor R W c	I	Baltimore
Piper J M	D	Newton
Ralph Daniel	C	Peabody
Ratliff J A	D	Columbus
Reece Solomon	E	Jackson
Sayers Martin	H	McCune
Smith James F	K	Burdon
Stonebraker Silas s	E	Topsy
Stonebraker Adam c	E	Topsy
Stonebraker J R	E	Salina
Stout Thomas s	G	Elk Falls
Schell Isaac N	D	Mound City
Vickers James A	D	Wheatland
Vickroy Geo W	E	Cleveland
Weaver C H 1st s	D	Concordia
White B F	A	Ova
White Harrison	F	Auburn
Wright M D 1st lt	D	Elk City

ONE HUNDRED AND FORTY EIGHTH IN-
FANTRY, ONE YEAR'S SERVICE

Colonel, Nicholas R Buckle.

Ard J W	E	Osage
Baliff E H s	F	Robinson or Waterville
Baliff O W	F	Good Intent
Bartee Wm	K	Popcorn
Blaisdell Major	A	Wichita
Bradshaw Geo s	F	Topeka
Brown J H	E	Labette City
Brunnemer Isaac	E	Independence
Brunnemer J O	E	Jewell
Burks James S s	C	Peabody
Chamberlain Wm	A	Hutchinson
Curtis R M capt	C	Topeka
Davis D M	E	Concordia
Davis H R	H	Cletona
Fike D S major	E	Winfield
Fuller D F	B	Comanche
Hargrave Wm lt	B	Cedarvale
Helms G W	H	Reese
Hollingsworth Ira	E	Elk Falls
Hoover John H c	A	Corinth

Name	Co.	Place
Jarret Michael	H	Baxter Springs
Lirgenfelter A	H	Ashland
Lippert A C	F	LaCrosse
McDaniel H C	H	Minneapolis
Norris Alfred	E	Burrton
Pattison Fred	D	Edgerton
Phipps T L R	I	Long Island
Poor Edward	C	Minerva
Prescott Ivy 1st lt	E	Mound Valley
Roth Adam	I	Scranton
Rudd Bryant	B	Coyville
Runyan John	K	Independence
Ryan Wm	D	Weir City
Saunders T	A	Aubrey
Stewart I J	B	Wellington
Stipp J W	K	Urbana
Swartz J H	D	Hartford
Swartz Ed	D	Hartford
Vessels Thos	I	Castleton
West Louis	E	Ottawa

ONE HUNDRED AND FORTY-NINTH INFANTRY, ONE YEARS SERVICE.

Col. Wm. A. Fairbanks.

Name	Co.	Place
Brown Thomas	F	Hutchinson
Burnett J M c	G	South Mound
Burnett Virgil	G	Osage Mission
Cookerly W M c	H	Topeka
Cox Alexander c	C	North Topeka
Cutler G W	B	Hobart
Davis John H	I	Pomona
Dittemore T E c	D	Eureka
Dowdell J S capt	E	North Topeka
Gilbert N W	K	Bulls City
Gilmore L 1st s	F	Parsons
Goss J M asst surg		Anthony
Grahem J	G	Fulton
Greenwell Alex c	C	Sedgwick City
Hadley Allen	K	Crainville
Hammon H E	A	Altamont
Howell A J	F	Farlington
Hubbell Isaac c	F	Chetopa
Humphreys J W 1st lt	I	Mulberry Grove
Inman A M	F	Maud
Jones Asher O	E	Tecumseh
Jones James J	C	Parsons
Karnes Wm A	E	Sidney
Kelley A J c	G	Arlington
Kent Isaac	K	Clyde
Lassee E	F	Parsons
Mahan I C 1st lt	A	Fordham
Mann Wm	K	Wilder
Mattocks H T	C	Maywood
Michler Jacob	K	Baxter Springs
Mounts Wm A	D	Wilsey
Oliphant A S	H	Columbus
Phillips M R c	D	Independence
Pinkston Jesse	D	Liberty
Rader John B	D	Kelso
Reynolds A	G	Easton
Schrants S c	F	Truman
Scott Stephen	E	Muscotah
Short W H	G	Junction City
Smart J S	I	Lamonts Hill
Smart R D	I	Dragoon
Spencer J J	I	Greeley
Staats W F	A	Emporia
Stephens W S A C	H	Prescott
Stratton H D	G	Carbondale
Thompson J S	E	McCune
Tippin R A	I	Garnett

Taylor B W		Telmo
Vaugh S		Independence
Work Geo W	D	North Cedar
Zellers Daniel	D	Safford

ONE HUNDRED AND FIFTIETH INFANTRY,
ONE YEAR'S SERVICE.
Colonel, Marsh B Taylor.

Babb W H s	I	Waco
Baldwin John	C	Cherryvale
Bonebrake Ezra	H	Altamont
Bray Isaac	F	Yates Center
Byers David	F	Winfield
Chenoweth J M	A	South Haven
Chenoweth W S	A	South Haven
Conoan Frank com s		Eldorado
Cornell Wm	I	Cherryvale
Davenport Wm	I	Baxter Springs
Fross Geo W	D	Plum Grove
Fisher Geo W	D	Topeka
Fritz Enos	E	Yates Center
Fulton Wm F	F	Bronson
Galbreath M lt	E	Topeka
Goble John	A	Kirwin
Harvey Samuel	H	Liberty
Haynes R H	D	Keene
Holstein S L	G	Elsinore
Howey J S	F	Topeka
Humes Thos J	C	Portis
Kiff A C	H	Haworth
Larvo J P c	A	Waco
McVicar J R	A	Wichita
Miller A B	B	Kinec
Miller Aaron H	H	Mound Valley
Monihan Jerry	K	Seeley
Moorhead H B	A	Waco
Parsons B F	C	Fawn Creek
Pennington E W	I	Chetops
Phillips W F	F	Burrton
Pugh Isaac W	B	Halstead
Renick M F	H	Cherryvale
Rizer Philip	B	Eldorado
Sharp John S	B	Delhi
Sleppy George c	E	Wade
Smith J D	K	Piqua
Spillman John	I	Monmouth
Storms Owen	H	Ottawa
Stufflebaum H	I	Eldorado
Swayze David	G	Topeka
Thompson J T	A	Harper
Tucker J I	H	Salina
Tyler John	H	Junction City
While Wm	G	Neodesha
Wimmers Wm	G	Louisville

ONE HUNDRED AND FIFTY FIRST INFANTRY,
ONE YEAR'S SERVICE.
Colonel, Joshua Healy.

Allen O M	B	Hopewell
Beiber J W c	E	Norton
Berry John	D	Ridgeway
Bonestead A H	E	Centralia
Blacksome Geo W	I	Wilson
Clark Geo	E	Haddam
Copeland G R	A	Fawn Creek
Cox Geo W	H	Oneida
Cudney Chas	K	Hubbell, Neb
Demond E J	K	Ross

Doud W E	F	Eureka
Evans B R	E	Yates Center
Evans R B	E	Middleton
Farnham John		Garnett
Fisher Geo W	D	Topeka
Groat R R	D	Madison
Hagerman G V	A	Bremer
Hart F A	H	Vine Creek
Haynes A B	B	Argentine
Hilderly David		Onaga
Hight Jacob	D	Arkansas City
Hill John T c	I	Dunn
Kenover Elijah	H	Hutchinson
Keyes W H	C	Galva
Larabee Frank	E	Haddam
Larabee Theodore	E	Haddam
Lewis J F c	I	Dennis
Lichtenberger J H	K	Clyde
Lynde Loreu W	E	Clifton
Marshall J B lt	B	Olathe
Martindale J c	C	Coyville, Manhattan
McCartey E T c	E	La Cygne
McVicar J R	A	Wichita
Miller Taylor	C	Salina
Miller D S	D	Hepler or Walnut
Milner Thomas	B	Chester, Neb
Myers James G	K	Le Roy
Moon J E 1st lt	G	Hiawatha
Nimrod T A	H	Burden
Rakestrow Job	K	Osborne
Rice S C	H	Arkansas City
Rosecrans F M		Myrtle
Sholl J S	B	Hubbell, Neb
Simison J H c	F	Wichita
Simpson E P	K	Blue Mound
Speer Edwards	B	Manhattan
Saward J W	F	Mound City
Sargent A N	F	Iola
Stahlmaker W H lt	F	Kansas City, Mo
Tanquary N M c	C	Neodesha
Warne H	H	Reno Center
Watkins Thomas	F	Wichita
Watts F M	E	Sedgwick
White D A capt	I	Eudora
Wood J A	E	Burr Oak
Woolpert S B	C	Irving
Wooster J	B	Ionia
Van Slyke A W lt	E	Yates Center

ONE—HUNDRED AND FIFTY SECOND IN
FANTRY, ONE YEAR'S SERVICE.

Colonel, Whedon W. Griswold.

Abbey G J c	C	Xenia
Adair Thos c	B	Moline
Bailey Alex	H	Rex
Bason W W	D	Neodesha
Banmback Jacob c	E	Detroit
Boyd Cornelius M lt	E	Winfield
Brinley Luke	F	Goddard
Carter H C	C	Eldorado
Caseberr Jay	B	Waterville
Chivington O C	E	Blendon
Circle I F	I	Prosper
Cooper Leonard	C	Atchison
Cory Alonzo	A	Hadley
Cory A J	A	Hadley
Crooks Albert	H	Mayday
Davids Freeman	B	Hiawatha
Dodge C H c	C	Cottonwood Falls

Emenizer Adam	H	Elk City
Faulkner F J	D	Irving
Foguell S	G	Grand Haven
French T E	E	Eskridge
Gardner Geo	C	Hiawatha
George J M	C	Altoona
Goff Elijah	A	Millwood
Grover J C	G	Iuka
Harzog Moses c	A	Hardilie
Haskins C T	E	Canon City, Col.
Hoover Reuben	B	Norton
Huff John	F	Crestline
Hunt Joshua	K	Fairfax
Kales Geo W	I	Almena
Kesling John	I	Neodesha
Knight Thos	E	St George
Kinsey G R	B	Eskridge
Lobdall W	G	Le Compton
Makenson J H s	B	Plumb
Makenson C E	B	Cana
Medland Hiram	E	Trenton
Onden John	B	Osborne City
Parsons Seymour	K	Equity
Potts B M	B	Edna
Prongh Simon	E	Parsons
Rima J H	E	Smith Center
Sherwin J F hosp st'd		Elk Falls
Shyre C D	C	Eldorado
Sisk N	D	De Witt
Skinner J L	B	Centralia
Smith F P	E	Edna
Stevens H J	D	Derby
Summerville J S c	D	Oxford
Thomas Eli	D	Kirwin
Walters Simon	C	Oak Hill
Weiler Jasper lt	H	Kingman
Wells J F c	C	Bellville
Widup Cyru. S	I	Ripon
Yeager E	B	Rose Hill
York J H	G	Girard

ONE HUNDRED FIFTY-THIRD INFANTRY

ONE YEAR'S SERVICE.

Colonel—Olivet H. P. Carey.

Abbott F M	F	Urbana
Becker J T lt	B	Glen Elder
Bridwell A J	F	Red Bud
Branan T J	H	Grantville
Burk S R	F	Corning
Campbell Wm	I	Mound Valley
Cary David	B	Harper
Coulter Cyrus	G	Burlington
Cramly Ira c	E	Fredonia
Chalmers G W	A	Ossawatomie
Gan R L	H	Irving
Haines E i C	A	Millerton
Hall B dev	G	Peabody
Hartman J R	K	Morrill
Heath J C	B	Muscotah
Hiatt E M s	G	Mound City
Kindlesparger J R	G	Topsy
Lamburn O H P	H	Abilene
Line J B	D	Augusta
Malsburg J B 1st s	F	Erie
Marshall Joseph	C	Lucas
Mather J K	D	Marion or Marie
Miller E P	C	Morrill
Mitten J D s	A	Wilson
Parker S W	I	Keighley

Perrett Fred	F	Mulvane
Pitts I L	I	Dowell
Pressler J K P	B	Carson
Ruess J F lt	D	Waynesburg, Mo
Ruse Aaron P	C	Atchison
Schloner J J	G	Augusta
Scott J A	G	Cora
Seward E H c	H	Sterling
Taylor J D	B	Eureka
Tillury W M 1st s	B	Lotta
Wagner G W	D	Erie

ONE . HUNDRED AND FIFTY-FOURTH INFANTRY, ONE YEARS SERVICE.

Col. Frank Wilcox.

Allen Wm	H		Cloverdale
Bates R H	A		Beloit
Bever Stephen	C		Monmouth
Brown W H 1st lt	I		Wyandotte
Bryan J M lt	H		Sedan
Byn m P L	B		Wellington
Cox Philander	H		Longton
Crain Cyrus	C		Columbus
Cruse G W	B		Cherryvale
Dorman James	B		East Wolf
Douglas S V	F		Grenola
Edmundson G W	H		Ottawa
Fouts John	F		Kingman
Goldsborough H L 1st lt	B		Lorette
Grimes S H c	B		Fall River
Harvey Wm S	D		Garnett
Job John S	K		Wellsville
Kersey Cyrenius	A		Aliceville
Larrimore Geo	I		Dodge City
Lawrence B E	I		Lyons
Lucas I B	F		Elk City
Martin W W lt	B		Ft Scott
McFeters W C	D		Girard
Mercer Wm	H		Arkansas City
Nicholas W H	G		Phillipsburg
Riley John	D		Mayview
Robbins Reddin	C		Ottawa
Shank J	E		Wichita
Shipman H H	C		Girard
Shreves J W	E		Augusta
Smith J M	E		Fawn Creek
Snavely J B	B		Millerton
Thomas Allen	I		Brooks
Thompson J W	G		Rock
Uhler Henry	B		Jamestown
Utz Josephus	F		Sedgwick City
Wilkins J W	D		Independence
Windbigler Wm	E		Mound Valley
Woodring H c	B		Elk City

ONE HUNDRED AND FIFTY-FIFTH INFANTRY
ONE YEAR'S SERVICE.

Colonel, John M. Wilson.

Anderson Arch d	A	West Asher
Bailey T J	A	Eureka
Baker Caleb	F	Avon
Bell Chas H	I	Oneida
Bowman Jonathan	D	Strawn
Burge O P	B	Haddam
Carson P T	E	Dennis
Carson J R	E	Dennis
Case Albert	A	Meriden
Cronmiller Jacob	D	Somerset

Name	Co.	Place
Frizzell J G	F	Laura
Fulmer Marion	B	Concordia
Hann Benj	K	Middle Branch
Harris W J	I	Cedron
Hoffley W H	A	Osage Mission
Hood S H c	G	Erie
Humbert H	A	Emporia
James F A	D	Andover
Koons W L	G	Cambridge
Kessler W L	A	Ripon
Knofflouch J	A	Blendon
Penwell H C	I	Scandia
Reimenschnider C	H	Ionia
Reeves C H	B	Haddam
Ritchie W H	D	Nickerson
Stoneberger John	K	Fordham
Stuck J M	H	Pleasant Run
Summers L N	E	Kansas City, Mo
Totten J J lt	F	Dorrance
Welch E B	C	Olathe
Welch E C	C	Armourdale
Williams T 1st s	A	Barton
Wilson Isaiah	H	Hubbel, Neb
Wright S S	E	Lyons
Wyant Isaac	E	Severy

ONE HUNDRED AND FIFTY-SIXTH INFAN-
TRY, ONE YEAR'S SERVICE.

Lt. Col. Chas. M. Smith.

Name	Co.	Place
Benedict J L	B	Elk Falls
Burson J C	E	Louisburg
Bussinger J T	E	Sweet Home
Clymer J V capt	B	Hutchinson
Ellis Robt	E	Delta
French T E	E	Eskridge
Funkhouser J G	E	Xenia
Hamilton J B	B	Ft Scott
Harrison J W	A	Vidette
Knee A R	A	Irving
Mattox N B	D	Dora or Coffeyville
Meloy Daniel	B	Cato
Morgan J H	A	Baltimore
Ogle Lewis A	B	Michigan Valley
Rea John A s	C	Hutchinson
Smith Simon	C	Greenleaf
Walden A G	B	Wichita
Walker J P	C	Turon

LAMB'S INDEPENDENT CAVALRY COMPANY,
ONE YEAR'S SERVICE.

Name	Co.	Place
Brown J L	A	Yates Center
Burt S R	F	Corning
Caffas G W c	A	Iuka
Damond	K	Rose
Herrod Benj s	H	Winfield

FIRST BATTERY INDIANA LIGHT ARTILLERY,
THREE YEARS' SERVICE.

Brown Ed m	Yates Center
Cooprider Wm	McPherson
Cromwell G P	Mayview
Ehret John c	St John
Kimberlin Geo	Ft Scott
McClure Jacob S	Topeka
Springer Robert	Chase

SECOND INDIANA BATTERY, LIGHT
ARTILLERY.

Clark S W	Minersville
Cooper John	Box City

Freed Thos J	Sabetha
Jones John M	Welcome
McNeer Val	Topeka
Orner S O s	Topeka
Rabb Geo J	Cadmus
Roberts W W	Clay Center
Wahans Fred	Millwood

THIRD INDIANA BATTERY, LIGHT ARTILLERY.

Boone W L	Salina
Elliott W W	Wyandotte
Evans W R bugler	Salina
Gwinn W H c	Wellsville
Johnes W O	Mankato
Kuhn Sam'l artificer	Great Bend
Main Leonard	Pleasanton
Osborn Madison c	Phillipsburg
Pool Geo L c	Beloit
Riddle F M	Blue Rapids
Stoll D W	Rossville
Smith N H	Empire City

FOURTH INDIANA BATTERY, LIGHT ARTILLERY, THREE YEARS' SERVICE.

Dawson W	Holton
Graves Samuel	Cecil
Haines D W 1st s	Galena
Hodson John	Urbana
Hooker E H	Barnesville
Hoskins H R	Liberty
McDaniel T W	Lane
Pitts B F	Cedarvale
Sharp Geo	Brush Creek
Tobias Norwood	Manhattan

FIFTH INDIANA BATTERY.

Beckner Joel	Brantford
Donly J H s	Hiawatha
Egner John	North Lawrence
Galentine H	Moline
Henry Wm c	Lindsburg
Shaffer C	Independence
Shoup Sol	Neodesha
Walton J C	Lawrence
Weckerlin H J	Cottonwood Falls

SIXTH INDIANA BATTERY.

Crayton Campbell	Holton
Crisman Peter	Bennington
Stevenson H G	Glasco
Saunders J H	Osawkee
Zeigler Franz c	Frankfort

SEVENTH INDIANA BATTERY, LIGHT ARTILLERY, THREE YEARS

Carmichael M A	Colon
James J T	Rossville
James Wm L	Rossville
Galentine H	Moline
Martin J F c	Raymond
McCloskey R W	Lyons
Rhodes B	Neosho Falls
Robinson J W	Burrton
Thompson J M	Independence
Weckerlin H J	Cottonwood Falls

EIGHTH INDIANA BATTERY, LIGHT ARTILLERY, THREE YEARS.

Evans H S	Wilsey or Adams Peak
Harlan Zimri	Girard

McCloskey R W   Lyons
Van Sickle A J   Stafford
Young Wm   Carbondale

NINTH INDIANA BATTERY, LIGHT ARTILLERY, THREE YEARS.

Connelly J D   Udall
Ellott Joel   Wade
Fullerton John S   Black Jack
McKinsey G W c   Coffeyville
Porter B A   Cherryvale
Swearengen J P s   Iola

TENTH INDIANA BATTERY, LIGHT ARTILLERY, THREE YEARS.

Carnahan J L   Pleasanton
Davis J C   Greenleaf
De Spain J H c   Council Grove
Maltby Geo H   McPherson

ELEVENTH INDIANA BATTERY, LIGHT ARTILLERY, THREE YEARS.

Gillock T C s   Hutchinson
Jones J L   Venango
Linges C   Ft Scott
Shofer James   Osage Mission
Shuler Wm   Lyons
Totten A c   Osage City

TWELFTH INDIANA BATTERY, LIGHT ARTILLERY, THREE YEARS.

Dawson Wm   Holton
Heller T J   Cawker City
Webster W E   Falley Falls

THIRTEENTH INDIANA BATTERY, LIGHT ARTILLERY, THREE YEARS

Bonham 1st s   Newton
Belt A G   Bona Springs
Clark Ira c   Asherville
Cooper James P 2d lt   Douglas
Crowley J   Concordia
Crum A J   Burden
Dever Jesse   Clay Center or Springfield
Foster J W   Hunnewell
Hubbell J C   Fall River
Mitchell J W   El Dorado
Snyder John c   Moline
Thompson Alex   Peoria
Waas W H   Fredonia

FOURTEENTH INDIANA BATTERY, LIGHT ARTILLERY, THREE YEARS.

Creators F M   Oswego
Goodarick D C   Paola
Guess J F   Twin Creek
Michaels Henry   Osawkee
Tyler E C 2d lt   Pleasanton
White F P   Ottawa
Whiteside G P   Topeka

FIFTEENTH INDIANA BATTERY, LIGHT ARTILLERY, THREE YEARS.

Freeman Wm H   Hutchinson
Hartman Chas s   Seneca
Kenworthy D C   Sternerton
Lanning Joel   Longton
Painter D F   Newton
Pearman S c   Sabetha

rerry B F   McLouth
Smith Chas O   Harbine

SIXTEENTH INDIANA BATTERY. LIGHT ARTILLERY, THREE YEARS.

Bartley Newton	Matanzas
Harper J H	Wichita
Hull Jonathan	Osawkee
Krons Urias c	Dodge City
Orb F J	Coffeyville
Pate S J	West Creek
Patton Madison c	Independence
Pierce Geo M	Larned
Smith J C	Parsons
Underhill N H	LeRoy

SEVENTEENTH INDIANA BATTERY, LIGHT ARTILLERY, THREE YEARS.

Hawkins H C s	Parsons
Hutchinson David	Melvern
Shomar Peter wagoner	Pittsburg
Weld Henry	Delhi

EIGHTEENTH INDIANA BATTERY. LIGHT ARTILLERY, THREE YEARS.

Aldridge Wm	Howard
Barr M J s	Sterling
Beck M M capt	Holton
Davis Chas E	Hallowell
Hamer John	Leonardville
McBroom E J	Girard
Scott J A capt	Holton
Scott S H s	Holton or South Cedar
Scott John T	Holton
Shanks Truman	Solomon
Yates J M	Leavenworth

NINETEENTH INDIANA BATTERY, LIGHT ARTILLERY, THREE YEARS.

Brown C T	Dodge City
Keeler Clinton lt	Emporia
Morgan A W	Carbondale
Peret James W artificer	Wetmore
Starbuck H C	Florence
Hooker E H	Barnesville

TWENTIETH INDIANA BATTERY. LIGHT ABTILLERY, THREE YEARS.

Byre Isaac	Ida
Chaplin P R	Geuda Springs
Day Enos	Sedgewick
Green John W	Moline
Grudel J H	Mount Liberty
Sellers J A	Hubbel

TWENTY-FIRST INDIANA BATTERY, LIGHT ARTILLERY — THREE YEARS

Andrews W W capt	Minneapolis
Best R F	Halstead
Elias Chas F	Conway
Evans James _	Scandia
Launrand A	Rossville
Lawson C A c	New Salem
Phillips James	Emporia
Ringold John	Morehead

TWENTY-SECOND INDIANA BATTERY, LIGHT ARTILLERY — THREE YEARS.

Coffman Isaac	Burlingame
Hardin A W	Gardner

Johnson B L	Canton
Kenton J L •	Larned
Lyons T L	Brookville
Winner J F	Fredonia

TWENTY–THIRD INDIANA BATTERY, LIGHT
ARTILLERY — THREE YEARS.

Henny Hiram	Columbus
Miller David	Ottawa
Musselwhite J W	Rantoul
Searl J C	Garnett

TWENTY – FOURTH INDIANA BATTERY,
LIGHT ARTILLERY, THREE YEARS.

Allen Hiram lt	Williamsburg
Bennett J K artificer	Ellinwood
Bressett J E	Rossville
Carl Geo	
Codling C B	Wilson
Conrad Peter	Wilson
Julian M J c	Mankato
Mason J c	Arnold
McEwen Wm	Mound Valley
Standly M M	Silver Lake
Severt Aug c	Nickerson
Taylor W P s	Yates Center

TWENTY-FIFTH INDIANA BATTERY, LIGHT
ARTILLERY, THREE YEARS.

Barnes Geo W	Clyde
Farley T P lt	Valley Falls
Gilbert John	Deerton
Saunders G W	Spearville

TWENTY-SIXTH INDIANA BATTERY, LIGHT
ARTILLERY, WILDER'S BATTERY,
THREE YEARS.

Bonebrake W H H	Abilene
Brickler J S	Burgeville
Brown B M	Huron
Hopkins J J	Chautauqua Valley
Metzzer J S	Minneapolis
Montgomery J C 1st lt	Lamar
Stewart R M	Troy
Withers S K 1st s	Topeka

IRREGULAR AND REGIMENTS UNKNOWN.

Adolph Jacob teamster		Veitsburg
Ball James M art		Burlington
Barber Lucius		Lawrence
Barker Noble q m's dpt		Minneapolis
Batroff Cal c C and M		Carbondale
Benger Henry		Chalk Mound
Bennett Theo E med dept		Topeka
Bleam D C		Quenemo
Bock Peter lt		Blend. n.
Blume P	B.	Buffalo
Bostic H C infantry		Carbondale
Brown S		Concordia
Brunning J A c		Centropolis
Bundram A J		Emporia
Burkey Howard		Atchison
Cambern S M capt A D C		Parsons
Card B F lt art		Emporia
Carter Peter U S C I		Wyandotte
Cherry J R	K	Nortonville
Chenoweth E	F	LeRoy
Connell G W	F	Neosho Rapids
Cox Jacob	B	Bross.

Craig James			Clay Center
Crisman G M	arty		Burlington
Crosby J M	I cav		Sutphens Mill
Daferty Jake	lt		Wichita
Daniel John			Wichita
Davis W J			Delphos
Deel F M			Brenham
DeSpain J H	c	B	Council Grove
Dill W W			Wichita
Dodson Wm	●		Armstrong
Duan W H			Wichita
East Charles			Kinsley
Eaton Reuben			Brenham
Engle E C			Nortonville
Farris J M	c	H	Stafford
Fisback H G		I	Milwaukee
Flack A J			LaBette
Forest C G		G	Woody
Foust Charles	cav		Hesper
Frazier W W			Pleasant Run
Fritz Valentine			Hymer
Gamble J			Elk Falls
Gillett John		C	Castleton
Glorus J A	capt	A	Wichita
Graham John	1st lt	art'y	Dexter
Gray Alex		I	Cuba
Gregg Martin		I	Wichita
Gregory John	art'y		Greenwich
Grimes H E			Naomi
Guthrie Hugh			South Cedar
Halderbraumer J M		H	Wilson
Hallestadt Elza		H	Eldorado
Hamer H		A	Neodesha
Hamilton H	c	D	Crestline
Hardin S C			Grenola
Harmden L			Melvern
Hensley W H	1st s	B	Iowaville
Hess Finley	cav		Ft Scott
Hetrick J L	s	G	Chetopa
Hicks J A			Hillside
Hinshaw I			Lyons
Hislop Thos	lt		Abilene
Hockett Matt		F	Lamar
Holden W G	lt		Ft Scott
Hooton H L		D	Cawker City
Hummer Wm			Emporia
Huston D A	cav		Akron
Hutchings J		A	Chetopa
Irwin S P	A		Lecompton
Jackson Wm F			Neosho Falls
Jerome John		I	Wichita
Johns J H	D		Humboldt
Johnson Alfred			Newton
Johnson G W		I	Newton
Johnson G E			Brenham
Jones Nathan	A		Neosho Falls
Kellam Aaron			Haworth
Kellar Jacob			Sedgewick
Kelley Mark	ma'or		Washington
Kennedy S W	art'y		Topeka
Kimball W L	hosp st'd		Wellington
Kinzie G	K		Padonia
Kinzey R	B		Eskridge
Kirby B F			Oswego
Kirk O D			Wichita
Knight J B			Pole
Knipe Wm	A		Garriso
Knoflnch A			Wichita
Long Enos			Clay Center
Long David		D, car	Carbondale
Magner Oren			Ladore

Mallatt A M			Oak Valley
Markell H D s	D, cav		Halstead
Marshall W J	E		Richmond
Marshall J A 2d ass't surg			Caney
Maine Harvey	C		Larned
Marts John s	E		Chapman
Massey J F			Kingman
McCaw S P			Hartford
McCoy F lt	E		Pleasanton
McCullough S			Grand View
McGraw W	cav		Lyle
McKee W H lt	art		Olathe
McKowen Jas	A		Louisville
McLain R s			Wichita
McNamara E	cav		Vallonia
Miller G F	A		Topeka
Miller T farrier	1st Eng's		Great Bend
Miller C W s	art'y		Emporia
Miller Arthur	F		Wells
Miller P R	art'y		Wichita
Milliken W J marine			Edna
Mitchell Daniel	A		La Cygne
Moon J G capt	K		Hiawatha
Moore E H s			Holton
Morgan A W			Lawrence
Myers Joseph			Valley Falls
Nelson Nathan	art'y		Fredonia
Newell J N			Burrton
Newport Fph			Olivet
Niebaum H s	I		Tonganoxie
Noble J E	B		Urbana
Norris N c	D		Cedarvale
North S P	I		Chautauqua Springs
Olinger John			Kinsley
Oliver J S			Waterloo
Osborne J E	.		Council Grove
Owens D S	C cav		Neodesha
Palmer Horace			Garnett
Parker D			Waterloo
Parson Wm	B		Marysville
Pearson A E 1st s	A		Burr Oak
Pennington D	I		Belle Plaine
Piety A H c			Topeka
Prentice Geo			Grenada
Postlethwaite T B			Wichita
Price Evan	G		Wichita
Proctor Discon	V R C		Atchison
Proctor John	E		Newton
Raider R			Belleville
Ramsey Isaac			Kingman
Rasure G W			Wellington
Reeves E			Salem
Renshaw A	art'y		Spring Side
Rhien Wm	I		Spring Valley
Rinard S Sigels' body guard			Topsy
Robinson W M Sturgis rifle cps			Windsor
Rochenbach C			Burden
Romine C	F		Lyndon
Rubottom A W	G		Red Clover
Sanyer E C	K		Longton
Saunders W F			Elk City
Schweek P F	H		Great Bend
Scott W H maj	P M		Huron
Scritchfield W T			Manhattan
Shafer J J	G		Jackson
hannon A R			Lincoln
Shannon J M			Mellville
Sharp J M	B		Wichita
Shore C C c	B		Oxford
Shuyler D M ...t lt	L		Sterling

Name			Place
Sells Anthony	A		Big Springs
Sinex W G	surg		Florence
Smith C C	D		Waseca
Smith A B	A		Plympton
Smith G B	c		Longton
Smith A R	A		Burrton
Smith G A	art'y		Ottumwa
Smith D A	wagon master		Everest
Sneathen G W	B		Erie
South Daniel	C		Goffs
South David	F	cav	Iola
Spears J	C		Wyandotte
Spears Wm	A		St Louis
Sanley Jehu			Topsy
Starns J J			Oswego
Stonebraker A	B		Tower Springs
Stifford Perry	s	G	Down:s
Sweeney Joshua	G		Randolph
Swigart A N			Carlyle
Taylor T E	C		Harrisonville
Teater Boyd			Eskridge
Therer J M			Crestline
Thomas W K	1st s	B	Ellis
Trullinger A	D		Mule Creek
Turner Thomas	G		Spring Creek
Turrell J R	eng'r cps		Leavenworth
Washburn E			Carbondale
Watson Asa	I		Redden
Watson R M			Valley Brook
Weber John	capt		Atchison
Ware J A			Severance
Weir James			Spearville
Wells R T			Dexter
Werner Alfred			Harper
Williams J			Parsons
Wilson Mark	H		Independence
Worth W W			Argonia
Youngman S H			Clay Center

MEXICAN WAR SOLDIERS FROM INDIANA
REGIMENTS, IN KANSAS.

Name		Place
Hovins S B	G 4th R	Strawn
Hier J D 1st lt c	D	Wathena
Hostetter B F	H 2d R	Farlinville
Hibbard L R	K 1st R	Smith Center
Kenyon W A c	G 3d R	Ackerland
La Fouser	C 1st R	Sedan
Moore E H s		Holton
McCaslin	C 3d R	Burlingame
Murray Wm	C 6th R	Kansas Center
Noblette F W	B 2d R	Dora
Newcomb R H	I 5th R	Farlinville
Owens Jonah	E 2d R	West Asher
Parr David	2d R	Beloit
Row Wm	A 5th R	Baxter Springs
Robinson W M	5th R	Windsor
Scott J H	2 1 R	Bennington
Smith W E L	1st R	Waterville
Short A J	D 5th R	Columbus
Sleeper V C	C 1st R	Medicine Lodge
Tevis I M	I 5th R	Topeka
Tibbett S L	G 1st R	La Harpe
Torrence R	H 3d R	Council Grove
Wiseman M	I 2d R	Strong City
Whiteman J	B 5th R	La Cygne

SAILORS AND MARINES FROM INDIANA IN
U. S NAVY IN KANSAS.

Name		Place
Cotton G C		Orie
Diehl L 2d mate, 1st marines		Chetopa

Gardner Casper	o s seaman		Hamline
Johnson F A	marines		Alma
Kelsey Scott			Topeka
Kimball			West Plains
McPhail D	seaman		Assaria
Pfaff M	marines		Emporia
Wright F			Lawrence

www.ingramcontent.com/pod-product-compliance
Lightning Source LLC
Chambersburg PA
CBHW030537270326
41927CB00008B/1419